Henry IV Part 1
by
William Shakespeare

Published in 1597

This Edition © Minerva Publishing, 2018

Cover Image: CC0 1.0 Universal (CC0 1.0)

ISBN: 9781983392887

Write us: contact@minervapublishing.net

MINERVA PUBLISHING

est. 2018

CONTENT

Act I

SCENE I. London. The palace.

Enter KING HENRY, LORD JOHN OF LANCASTER, the EARL of WESTMORELAND, SIR WALTER BLUNT, and others

KING HENRY IV

So shaken as we are, so wan with care,
 Find we a time for frighted peace to pant,
 And breathe short-winded accents of new broils
 To be commenced in strands afar remote.
 No more the thirsty entrance of this soil
 Shall daub her lips with her own children's blood;
 Nor more shall trenching war channel her fields,
 Nor bruise her flowerets with the armed hoofs
 Of hostile paces: those opposed eyes,
 Which, like the meteors of a troubled heaven,
 All of one nature, of one substance bred,
 Did lately meet in the intestine shock
 And furious close of civil butchery
 Shall now, in mutual well-beseeming ranks,
 March all one way and be no more opposed
 Against acquaintance, kindred and allies:
 The edge of war, like an ill-sheathed knife,
 No more shall cut his master. Therefore, friends,
 As far as to the sepulchre of Christ,
 Whose soldier now, under whose blessed cross
 We are impressed and engaged to fight,
 Forthwith a power of English shall we levy;
 Whose arms were moulded in their mothers' womb
 To chase these pagans in those holy fields
 Over whose acres walk'd those blessed feet
 Which fourteen hundred years ago were nail'd
 For our advantage on the bitter cross.
 But this our purpose now is twelve month old,
 And bootless 'tis to tell you we will go:
 Therefore we meet not now. Then let me hear

4

Of you, my gentle cousin Westmoreland,
What yesternight our council did decree
In forwarding this dear expedience.
WESTMORELAND
My liege, this haste was hot in question,
And many limits of the charge set down
But yesternight: when all athwart there came
A post from Wales loaden with heavy news;
Whose worst was, that the noble Mortimer,
Leading the men of Herefordshire to fight
Against the irregular and wild Glendower,
Was by the rude hands of that Welshman taken,
A thousand of his people butchered;
Upon whose dead corpse there was such misuse,
Such beastly shameless transformation,
By those Welshwomen done as may not be
Without much shame retold or spoken of.
KING HENRY IV
It seems then that the tidings of this broil
Brake off our business for the Holy Land.
WESTMORELAND
This match'd with other did, my gracious lord;
For more uneven and unwelcome news
Came from the north and thus it did import:
On Holy-rood day, the gallant Hotspur there,
Young Harry Percy and brave Archibald,
That ever-valiant and approved Scot,
At Holmedon met,
Where they did spend a sad and bloody hour,
As by discharge of their artillery,
And shape of likelihood, the news was told;
For he that brought them, in the very heat
And pride of their contention did take horse,
Uncertain of the issue any way.
KING HENRY IV
Here is a dear, a true industrious friend,
Sir Walter Blunt, new lighted from his horse.
Stain'd with the variation of each soil
Betwixt that Holmedon and this seat of ours;
And he hath brought us smooth and welcome news.

5

The Earl of Douglas is discomfited:
Ten thousand bold Scots, two and twenty knights,
Balk'd in their own blood did Sir Walter see
On Holmedon's plains. Of prisoners, Hotspur took
Mordake the Earl of Fife, and eldest son
To beaten Douglas; and the Earl of Athol,
Of Murray, Angus, and Menteith:
And is not this an honourable spoil?
A gallant prize? ha, cousin, is it not?
>   **WESTMORELAND**
In faith,
It is a conquest for a prince to boast of.
>   **KING HENRY IV**
Yea, there thou makest me sad and makest me sin
In envy that my Lord Northumberland
Should be the father to so blest a son,
A son who is the theme of honour's tongue;
Amongst a grove, the very straightest plant;
Who is sweet Fortune's minion and her pride:
Whilst I, by looking on the praise of him,
See riot and dishonour stain the brow
Of my young Harry. O that it could be proved
That some night-tripping fairy had exchanged
In cradle-clothes our children where they lay,
And call'd mine Percy, his Plantagenet!
Then would I have his Harry, and he mine.
But let him from my thoughts. What think you, coz,
Of this young Percy's pride? the prisoners,
Which he in this adventure hath surprised,
To his own use he keeps; and sends me word,
I shall have none but Mordake Earl of Fife.
>   **WESTMORELAND**
This is his uncle's teaching; this is Worcester,
Malevolent to you in all aspects;
Which makes him prune himself, and bristle up
The crest of youth against your dignity.
>   **KING HENRY IV**
But I have sent for him to answer this;
And for this cause awhile we must neglect
Our holy purpose to Jerusalem.

Cousin, on Wednesday next our council we
Will hold at Windsor; so inform the lords:
But come yourself with speed to us again;
For more is to be said and to be done
Than out of anger can be uttered.
   WESTMORELAND
I will, my liege.
Exeunt

SCENE II. London. An apartment of the Prince's.

Enter the PRINCE OF WALES and FALSTAFF
FALSTAFF
Now, Hal, what time of day is it, lad?
PRINCE HENRY
Thou art so fat-witted, with drinking of old sack
and unbuttoning thee after supper and sleeping upon
benches after noon, that thou hast forgotten to
demand that truly which thou wouldst truly know.
What a devil hast thou to do with the time of the
day? Unless hours were cups of sack and minutes
capons and clocks the tongues of bawds and dials the
signs of leaping-houses and the blessed sun himself
a fair hot wench in flame-coloured taffeta, I see no
reason why thou shouldst be so superfluous to demand
the time of the day.
FALSTAFF
Indeed, you come near me now, Hal; for we that take
purses go by the moon and the seven stars, and not
by Phoebus, he,'that wandering knight so fair.' And,
I prithee, sweet wag, when thou art king, as, God
save thy grace,—majesty I should say, for grace
thou wilt have none,—
PRINCE HENRY
What, none?
FALSTAFF
No, by my troth, not so much as will serve to
prologue to an egg and butter.
PRINCE HENRY
Well, how then? come, roundly, roundly.
FALSTAFF
Marry, then, sweet wag, when thou art king, let not
us that are squires of the night's body be called
thieves of the day's beauty: let us be Diana's
foresters, gentlemen of the shade, minions of the
moon; and let men say we be men of good government,

8

being governed, as the sea is, by our noble and
chaste mistress the moon, under whose countenance we steal.

PRINCE HENRY

Thou sayest well, and it holds well too; for the
fortune of us that are the moon's men doth ebb and
flow like the sea, being governed, as the sea is,
by the moon. As, for proof, now: a purse of gold
most resolutely snatched on Monday night and most
dissolutely spent on Tuesday morning; got with
swearing 'Lay by' and spent with crying 'Bring in;'
now in as low an ebb as the foot of the ladder
and by and by in as high a flow as the ridge of the gallows.

FALSTAFF

By the Lord, thou sayest true, lad. And is not my
hostess of the tavern a most sweet wench?

PRINCE HENRY

As the honey of Hybla, my old lad of the castle. And
is not a buff jerkin a most sweet robe of durance?

FALSTAFF

How now, how now, mad wag! what, in thy quips and
thy quiddities? what a plague have I to do with a
buff jerkin?

PRINCE HENRY

Why, what a pox have I to do with my hostess of the tavern?

FALSTAFF

Well, thou hast called her to a reckoning many a
time and oft.

PRINCE HENRY

Did I ever call for thee to pay thy part?

FALSTAFF

No; I'll give thee thy due, thou hast paid all there.

PRINCE HENRY

Yea, and elsewhere, so far as my coin would stretch;
and where it would not, I have used my credit.

FALSTAFF

Yea, and so used it that were it not here apparent
that thou art heir apparent—But, I prithee, sweet
wag, shall there be gallows standing in England when
thou art king? and resolution thus fobbed as it is

with the rusty curb of old father antic the law? Do
not thou, when thou art king, hang a thief.

PRINCE HENRY

No; thou shalt.

FALSTAFF

Shall I? O rare! By the Lord, I'll be a brave judge.

PRINCE HENRY

Thou judgest false already: I mean, thou shalt have
the hanging of the thieves and so become a rare hangman.

FALSTAFF

Well, Hal, well; and in some sort it jumps with my
humour as well as waiting in the court, I can tell
you.

PRINCE HENRY

For obtaining of suits?

FALSTAFF

Yea, for obtaining of suits, whereof the hangman
hath no lean wardrobe. 'Sblood, I am as melancholy
as a gib cat or a lugged bear.

PRINCE HENRY

Or an old lion, or a lover's lute.

FALSTAFF

Yea, or the drone of a Lincolnshire bagpipe.

PRINCE HENRY

What sayest thou to a hare, or the melancholy of
Moor-ditch?

FALSTAFF

Thou hast the most unsavoury similes and art indeed
the most comparative, rascalliest, sweet young
prince. But, Hal, I prithee, trouble me no more
with vanity. I would to God thou and I knew where a
commodity of good names were to be bought. An old
lord of the council rated me the other day in the
street about you, sir, but I marked him not; and yet
he talked very wisely, but I regarded him not; and
yet he talked wisely, and in the street too.

PRINCE HENRY

Thou didst well; for wisdom cries out in the
streets, and no man regards it.

FALSTAFF

O, thou hast damnable iteration and art indeed able
to corrupt a saint. Thou hast done much harm upon
me, Hal; God forgive thee for it! Before I knew
thee, Hal, I knew nothing; and now am I, if a man
should speak truly, little better than one of the
wicked. I must give over this life, and I will give
it over: by the Lord, and I do not, I am a villain:
I'll be damned for never a king's son in
Christendom.

PRINCE HENRY

Where shall we take a purse tomorrow, Jack?

FALSTAFF

'Zounds, where thou wilt, lad; I'll make one; an I
do not, call me villain and baffle me.

PRINCE HENRY

I see a good amendment of life in thee; from praying
to purse-taking.

FALSTAFF

Why, Hal, 'tis my vocation, Hal; 'tis no sin for a
man to labour in his vocation.

Enter POINS

Poins! Now shall we know if Gadshill have set a
match. O, if men were to be saved by merit, what
hole in hell were hot enough for him? This is the
most omnipotent villain that ever cried 'Stand' to
a true man.

PRINCE HENRY

Good morrow, Ned.

POINS

Good morrow, sweet Hal. What says Monsieur Remorse?
what says Sir John Sack and Sugar? Jack! how
agrees the devil and thee about thy soul, that thou
soldest him on Good-Friday last for a cup of Madeira
and a cold capon's leg?

PRINCE HENRY

Sir John stands to his word, the devil shall have
his bargain; for he was never yet a breaker of
proverbs: he will give the devil his due.

POINS

Then art thou damned for keeping thy word with the devil.

PRINCE HENRY

Else he had been damned for cozening the devil.

POINS

But, my lads, my lads, to-morrow morning, by four
o'clock, early at Gadshill! there are pilgrims going
to Canterbury with rich offerings, and traders
riding to London with fat purses: I have vizards
for you all; you have horses for yourselves:
Gadshill lies to-night in Rochester: I have bespoke
supper to-morrow night in Eastcheap: we may do it
as secure as sleep. If you will go, I will stuff
your purses full of crowns; if you will not, tarry
at home and be hanged.

FALSTAFF

Hear ye, Yedward; if I tarry at home and go not,
I'll hang you for going.

POINS

You will, chops?

FALSTAFF

Hal, wilt thou make one?

PRINCE HENRY

Who, I rob? I a thief? not I, by my faith.

FALSTAFF

There's neither honesty, manhood, nor good
fellowship in thee, nor thou camest not of the blood
royal, if thou darest not stand for ten shillings.

PRINCE HENRY

Well then, once in my days I'll be a madcap.

FALSTAFF

Why, that's well said.

PRINCE HENRY

Well, come what will, I'll tarry at home.

FALSTAFF

By the Lord, I'll be a traitor then, when thou art king.

PRINCE HENRY

I care not.

POINS

Sir John, I prithee, leave the prince and me alone:
I will lay him down such reasons for this adventure
that he shall go.

FALSTAFF

Well, God give thee the spirit of persuasion and him
the ears of profiting, that what thou speakest may
move and what he hears may be believed, that the
true prince may, for recreation sake, prove a false
thief; for the poor abuses of the time want
countenance. Farewell: you shall find me in Eastcheap.

PRINCE HENRY

Farewell, thou latter spring! farewell, All-hallown summer!

Exit Falstaff

POINS

Now, my good sweet honey lord, ride with us
to-morrow: I have a jest to execute that I cannot
manage alone. Falstaff, Bardolph, Peto and Gadshill
shall rob those men that we have already waylaid:
yourself and I will not be there; and when they
have the booty, if you and I do not rob them, cut
this head off from my shoulders.

PRINCE HENRY

How shall we part with them in setting forth?

POINS

Why, we will set forth before or after them, and
appoint them a place of meeting, wherein it is at
our pleasure to fail, and then will they adventure
upon the exploit themselves; which they shall have
no sooner achieved, but we'll set upon them.

PRINCE HENRY

Yea, but 'tis like that they will know us by our
horses, by our habits and by every other
appointment, to be ourselves.

POINS

Tut! our horses they shall not see: I'll tie them
in the wood; our vizards we will change after we
leave them: and, sirrah, I have cases of buckram
for the nonce, to immask our noted outward garments.

PRINCE HENRY

Yea, but I doubt they will be too hard for us.

POINS

Well, for two of them, I know them to be as
true-bred cowards as ever turned back; and for the
third, if he fight longer than he sees reason, I'll
forswear arms. The virtue of this jest will be, the
incomprehensible lies that this same fat rogue will
tell us when we meet at supper: how thirty, at
least, he fought with; what wards, what blows, what
extremities he endured; and in the reproof of this
lies the jest.

PRINCE HENRY

Well, I'll go with thee: provide us all things
necessary and meet me to-morrow night in Eastcheap;
there I'll sup. Farewell.

POINS

Farewell, my lord.

Exit Poins

PRINCE HENRY

I know you all, and will awhile uphold
The unyoked humour of your idleness:
Yet herein will I imitate the sun,
Who doth permit the base contagious clouds
To smother up his beauty from the world,
That, when he please again to be himself,
Being wanted, he may be more wonder'd at,
By breaking through the foul and ugly mists
Of vapours that did seem to strangle him.
If all the year were playing holidays,
To sport would be as tedious as to work;
But when they seldom come, they wish'd for come,
And nothing pleaseth but rare accidents.
So, when this loose behavior I throw off
And pay the debt I never promised,
By how much better than my word I am,
By so much shall I falsify men's hopes;
And like bright metal on a sullen ground,
My reformation, glittering o'er my fault,
Shall show more goodly and attract more eyes

Than that which hath no foil to set it off.
I'll so offend, to make offence a skill;
Redeeming time when men think least I will.
Exit

SCENE III. London. The palace.

Enter the KING, NORTHUMBERLAND, WORCESTER, HOTSPUR,
SIR WALTER BLUNT, with others

KING HENRY IV

My blood hath been too cold and temperate,
 Unapt to stir at these indignities,
 And you have found me; for accordingly
 You tread upon my patience: but be sure
 I will from henceforth rather be myself,
 Mighty and to be fear'd, than my condition;
 Which hath been smooth as oil, soft as young down,
 And therefore lost that title of respect
 Which the proud soul ne'er pays but to the proud.

EARL OF WORCESTER

Our house, my sovereign liege, little deserves
 The scourge of greatness to be used on it;
 And that same greatness too which our own hands
 Have holp to make so portly.

NORTHUMBERLAND

My lord.—

KING HENRY IV

Worcester, get thee gone; for I do see
 Danger and disobedience in thine eye:
 O, sir, your presence is too bold and peremptory,
 And majesty might never yet endure
 The moody frontier of a servant brow.
 You have good leave to leave us: when we need
 Your use and counsel, we shall send for you.

Exit Worcester

You were about to speak.

To North

NORTHUMBERLAND

Yea, my good lord.
 Those prisoners in your highness' name demanded,
 Which Harry Percy here at Holmedon took,
 Were, as he says, not with such strength denied
 As is deliver'd to your majesty:

Either envy, therefore, or misprison
Is guilty of this fault and not my son.

   HOTSPUR

My liege, I did deny no prisoners.
But I remember, when the fight was done,
When I was dry with rage and extreme toil,
Breathless and faint, leaning upon my sword,
Came there a certain lord, neat, and trimly dress'd,
Fresh as a bridegroom; and his chin new reap'd
Show'd like a stubble-land at harvest-home;
He was perfumed like a milliner;
And 'twixt his finger and his thumb he held
A pouncet-box, which ever and anon
He gave his nose and took't away again;
Who therewith angry, when it next came there,
Took it in snuff; and still he smiled and talk'd,
And as the soldiers bore dead bodies by,
He call'd them untaught knaves, unmannerly,
To bring a slovenly unhandsome corse
Betwixt the wind and his nobility.
With many holiday and lady terms
He question'd me; amongst the rest, demanded
My prisoners in your majesty's behalf.
I then, all smarting with my wounds being cold,
To be so pester'd with a popinjay,
Out of my grief and my impatience,
Answer'd neglectingly I know not what,
He should or he should not; for he made me mad
To see him shine so brisk and smell so sweet
And talk so like a waiting-gentlewoman
Of guns and drums and wounds,—God save the mark!—
And telling me the sovereign'st thing on earth
Was parmaceti for an inward bruise;
And that it was great pity, so it was,
This villanous salt-petre should be digg'd
Out of the bowels of the harmless earth,
Which many a good tall fellow had destroy'd
So cowardly; and but for these vile guns,
He would himself have been a soldier.
This bald unjointed chat of his, my lord,

17

I answer'd indirectly, as I said;
And I beseech you, let not his report
Come current for an accusation
Betwixt my love and your high majesty.

SIR WALTER BLUNT

The circumstance consider'd, good my lord,
Whate'er Lord Harry Percy then had said
To such a person and in such a place,
At such a time, with all the rest retold,
May reasonably die and never rise
To do him wrong or any way impeach
What then he said, so he unsay it now.

KING HENRY IV

Why, yet he doth deny his prisoners,
But with proviso and exception,
That we at our own charge shall ransom straight
His brother-in-law, the foolish Mortimer;
Who, on my soul, hath wilfully betray'd
The lives of those that he did lead to fight
Against that great magician, damn'd Glendower,
Whose daughter, as we hear, the Earl of March
Hath lately married. Shall our coffers, then,
Be emptied to redeem a traitor home?
Shall we but treason? and indent with fears,
When they have lost and forfeited themselves?
No, on the barren mountains let him starve;
For I shall never hold that man my friend
Whose tongue shall ask me for one penny cost
To ransom home revolted Mortimer.

HOTSPUR

Revolted Mortimer!
He never did fall off, my sovereign liege,
But by the chance of war; to prove that true
Needs no more but one tongue for all those wounds,
Those mouthed wounds, which valiantly he took
When on the gentle Severn's sedgy bank,
In single opposition, hand to hand,
He did confound the best part of an hour
In changing hardiment with great Glendower:
Three times they breathed and three times did

they drink,
Upon agreement, of swift Severn's flood;
Who then, affrighted with their bloody looks,
Ran fearfully among the trembling reeds,
And hid his crisp head in the hollow bank,
Bloodstained with these valiant combatants.
Never did base and rotten policy
Colour her working with such deadly wounds;
Nor could the noble Mortimer
Receive so many, and all willingly:
Then let not him be slander'd with revolt.

KING HENRY IV

Thou dost belie him, Percy, thou dost belie him;
He never did encounter with Glendower:
I tell thee,
He durst as well have met the devil alone
As Owen Glendower for an enemy.
Art thou not ashamed? But, sirrah, henceforth
Let me not hear you speak of Mortimer:
Send me your prisoners with the speediest means,
Or you shall hear in such a kind from me
As will displease you. My Lord Northumberland,
We licence your departure with your son.
Send us your prisoners, or you will hear of it.
Exeunt King Henry, Blunt, and train

HOTSPUR

An if the devil come and roar for them,
I will not send them: I will after straight
And tell him so; for I will ease my heart,
Albeit I make a hazard of my head.

NORTHUMBERLAND

What, drunk with choler? stay and pause awhile:
Here comes your uncle.
Re-enter WORCESTER

HOTSPUR

Speak of Mortimer!
'Zounds, I will speak of him; and let my soul
Want mercy, if I do not join with him:
Yea, on his part I'll empty all these veins,
And shed my dear blood drop by drop in the dust,

But I will lift the down-trod Mortimer
As high in the air as this unthankful king,
As this ingrate and canker'd Bolingbroke.

NORTHUMBERLAND

Brother, the king hath made your nephew mad.

EARL OF WORCESTER

Who struck this heat up after I was gone?

HOTSPUR

He will, forsooth, have all my prisoners;
And when I urged the ransom once again
Of my wife's brother, then his cheek look'd pale,
And on my face he turn'd an eye of death,
Trembling even at the name of Mortimer.

EARL OF WORCESTER

I cannot blame him: was not he proclaim'd
By Richard that dead is the next of blood?

NORTHUMBERLAND

He was; I heard the proclamation:
And then it was when the unhappy king,
—Whose wrongs in us God pardon!—did set forth
Upon his Irish expedition;
From whence he intercepted did return
To be deposed and shortly murdered.

EARL OF WORCESTER

And for whose death we in the world's wide mouth
Live scandalized and foully spoken of.

HOTSPUR

But soft, I pray you; did King Richard then
Proclaim my brother Edmund Mortimer
Heir to the crown?

NORTHUMBERLAND

He did; myself did hear it.

HOTSPUR

Nay, then I cannot blame his cousin king,
That wished him on the barren mountains starve.
But shall it be that you, that set the crown
Upon the head of this forgetful man
And for his sake wear the detested blot
Of murderous subornation, shall it be,
That you a world of curses undergo,

Being the agents, or base second means,
The cords, the ladder, or the hangman rather?
O, pardon me that I descend so low,
To show the line and the predicament
Wherein you range under this subtle king;
Shall it for shame be spoken in these days,
Or fill up chronicles in time to come,
That men of your nobility and power
Did gage them both in an unjust behalf,
As both of you—God pardon it!—have done,
To put down Richard, that sweet lovely rose,
An plant this thorn, this canker, Bolingbroke?
And shall it in more shame be further spoken,
That you are fool'd, discarded and shook off
By him for whom these shames ye underwent?
No; yet time serves wherein you may redeem
Your banish'd honours and restore yourselves
Into the good thoughts of the world again,
Revenge the jeering and disdain'd contempt
Of this proud king, who studies day and night
To answer all the debt he owes to you
Even with the bloody payment of your deaths:
Therefore, I say—

EARL OF WORCESTER

Peace, cousin, say no more:
And now I will unclasp a secret book,
And to your quick-conceiving discontents
I'll read you matter deep and dangerous,
As full of peril and adventurous spirit
As to o'er-walk a current roaring loud
On the unsteadfast footing of a spear.

HOTSPUR

If he fall in, good night! or sink or swim:
Send danger from the east unto the west,
So honour cross it from the north to south,
And let them grapple: O, the blood more stirs
To rouse a lion than to start a hare!

NORTHUMBERLAND

Imagination of some great exploit
Drives him beyond the bounds of patience.

HOTSPUR

By heaven, methinks it were an easy leap,
 To pluck bright honour from the pale-faced moon,
 Or dive into the bottom of the deep,
 Where fathom-line could never touch the ground,
 And pluck up drowned honour by the locks;
 So he that doth redeem her thence might wear
 Without corrival, all her dignities:
 But out upon this half-faced fellowship!

EARL OF WORCESTER

He apprehends a world of figures here,
 But not the form of what he should attend.
 Good cousin, give me audience for a while.

HOTSPUR

I cry you mercy.

EARL OF WORCESTER

Those same noble Scots
 That are your prisoners,—

HOTSPUR

I'll keep them all;
 By God, he shall not have a Scot of them;
 No, if a Scot would save his soul, he shall not:
 I'll keep them, by this hand.

EARL OF WORCESTER

You start away
 And lend no ear unto my purposes.
 Those prisoners you shall keep.

HOTSPUR

Nay, I will; that's flat:
 He said he would not ransom Mortimer;
 Forbad my tongue to speak of Mortimer;
 But I will find him when he lies asleep,
 And in his ear I'll holla 'Mortimer!'
 Nay,
 I'll have a starling shall be taught to speak
 Nothing but 'Mortimer,' and give it him
 To keep his anger still in motion.

EARL OF WORCESTER

Hear you, cousin; a word.

HOTSPUR

All studies here I solemnly defy,
 Save how to gall and pinch this Bolingbroke:
 And that same sword-and-buckler Prince of Wales,
 But that I think his father loves him not
 And would be glad he met with some mischance,
 I would have him poison'd with a pot of ale.

EARL OF WORCESTER

Farewell, kinsman: I'll talk to you
 When you are better temper'd to attend.

NORTHUMBERLAND

Why, what a wasp-stung and impatient fool
 Art thou to break into this woman's mood,
 Tying thine ear to no tongue but thine own!

HOTSPUR

Why, look you, I am whipp'd and scourged with rods,
 Nettled and stung with pismires, when I hear
 Of this vile politician, Bolingbroke.
 In Richard's time,—what do you call the place?—
 A plague upon it, it is in Gloucestershire;
 'Twas where the madcap duke his uncle kept,
 His uncle York; where I first bow'd my knee
 Unto this king of smiles, this Bolingbroke,—
 'Sblood!—
 When you and he came back from Ravenspurgh.

NORTHUMBERLAND

At Berkley castle.

HOTSPUR

You say true:
 Why, what a candy deal of courtesy
 This fawning greyhound then did proffer me!
 Look,'when his infant fortune came to age,'
 And 'gentle Harry Percy,' and 'kind cousin;'
 O, the devil take such cozeners! God forgive me!
 Good uncle, tell your tale; I have done.

EARL OF WORCESTER

Nay, if you have not, to it again;
 We will stay your leisure.

HOTSPUR

I have done, i' faith.

EARL OF WORCESTER

Then once more to your Scottish prisoners.
Deliver them up without their ransom straight,
And make the Douglas' son your only mean
For powers in Scotland; which, for divers reasons
Which I shall send you written, be assured,
Will easily be granted. You, my lord,

To Northumberland

Your son in Scotland being thus employ'd,
Shall secretly into the bosom creep
Of that same noble prelate, well beloved,
The archbishop.

HOTSPUR

Of York, is it not?

EARL OF WORCESTER

True; who bears hard
His brother's death at Bristol, the Lord Scroop.
I speak not this in estimation,
As what I think might be, but what I know
Is ruminated, plotted and set down,
And only stays but to behold the face
Of that occasion that shall bring it on.

HOTSPUR

I smell it: upon my life, it will do well.

NORTHUMBERLAND

Before the game is afoot, thou still let'st slip.

HOTSPUR

Why, it cannot choose but be a noble plot;
And then the power of Scotland and of York,
To join with Mortimer, ha?

EARL OF WORCESTER

And so they shall.

HOTSPUR

In faith, it is exceedingly well aim'd.

EARL OF WORCESTER

And 'tis no little reason bids us speed,
To save our heads by raising of a head;
For, bear ourselves as even as we can,
The king will always think him in our debt,
And think we think ourselves unsatisfied,

Till he hath found a time to pay us home:
And see already how he doth begin
To make us strangers to his looks of love.
   HOTSPUR
He does, he does: we'll be revenged on him.
   EARL OF WORCESTER
Cousin, farewell: no further go in this
   Than I by letters shall direct your course.
   When time is ripe, which will be suddenly,
   I'll steal to Glendower and Lord Mortimer;
   Where you and Douglas and our powers at once,
   As I will fashion it, shall happily meet,
   To bear our fortunes in our own strong arms,
   Which now we hold at much uncertainty.
   NORTHUMBERLAND
Farewell, good brother: we shall thrive, I trust.
   HOTSPUR
Uncle, Adieu: O, let the hours be short
   Till fields and blows and groans applaud our sport!
Exeunt

Act II

SCENE I. Rochester. An inn yard.

Enter a Carrier with a lantern in his hand
First Carrier
Heigh-ho! an it be not four by the day, I'll be
 hanged: Charles' wain is over the new chimney, and
 yet our horse not packed. What, ostler!
Ostler
[Within] Anon, anon.
First Carrier
I prithee, Tom, beat Cut's saddle, put a few flocks
 in the point; poor jade, is wrung in the withers out
 of all cess.
Enter another Carrier
Second Carrier
Peas and beans are as dank here as a dog, and that
 is the next way to give poor jades the bots: this
 house is turned upside down since Robin Ostler died.
First Carrier
Poor fellow, never joyed since the price of oats
 rose; it was the death of him.
Second Carrier
I think this be the most villanous house in all
 London road for fleas: I am stung like a tench.
First Carrier
Like a tench! by the mass, there is ne'er a king
 christen could be better bit than I have been since
 the first cock.
Second Carrier
Why, they will allow us ne'er a jordan, and then we
 leak in your chimney; and your chamber-lie breeds
 fleas like a loach.
First Carrier
What, ostler! come away and be hanged!

26

Second Carrier

I have a gammon of bacon and two razors of ginger,
to be delivered as far as Charing-cross.

First Carrier

God's body! the turkeys in my pannier are quite
starved. What, ostler! A plague on thee! hast thou
never an eye in thy head? canst not hear? An
'twere not as good deed as drink, to break the pate
on thee, I am a very villain. Come, and be hanged!
hast thou no faith in thee?

Enter GADSHILL

GADSHILL

Good morrow, carriers. What's o'clock?

First Carrier

I think it be two o'clock.

GADSHILL

I pray thee lend me thy lantern, to see my gelding
in the stable.

First Carrier

Nay, by God, soft; I know a trick worth two of that, i' faith.

GADSHILL

I pray thee, lend me thine.

Second Carrier

Ay, when? can'st tell? Lend me thy lantern, quoth
he? marry, I'll see thee hanged first.

GADSHILL

Sirrah carrier, what time do you mean to come to London?

Second Carrier

Time enough to go to bed with a candle, I warrant
thee. Come, neighbour Mugs, we'll call up the
gentleman: they will along with company, for they
have great charge.

Exeunt carriers

GADSHILL

What, ho! chamberlain!

Chamberlain

[Within] At hand, quoth pick-purse.

GADSHILL

That's even as fair as—at hand, quoth the
chamberlain; for thou variest no more from picking

of purses than giving direction doth from labouring;
thou layest the plot how.

Enter Chamberlain

Chamberlain

Good morrow, Master Gadshill. It holds current that
I told you yesternight: there's a franklin in the
wild of Kent hath brought three hundred marks with
him in gold: I heard him tell it to one of his
company last night at supper; a kind of auditor; one
that hath abundance of charge too, God knows what.
They are up already, and call for eggs and butter;
they will away presently.

GADSHILL

Sirrah, if they meet not with Saint Nicholas'
clerks, I'll give thee this neck.

Chamberlain

No, I'll none of it: I pray thee keep that for the
hangman; for I know thou worshippest St. Nicholas
as truly as a man of falsehood may.

GADSHILL

What talkest thou to me of the hangman? if I hang,
I'll make a fat pair of gallows; for if I hang, old
Sir John hangs with me, and thou knowest he is no
starveling. Tut! there are other Trojans that thou
dreamest not of, the which for sport sake are
content to do the profession some grace; that would,
if matters should be looked into, for their own
credit sake, make all whole. I am joined with no
foot-land rakers, no long-staff sixpenny strikers,
none of these mad mustachio purple-hued malt-worms;
but with nobility and tranquillity, burgomasters and
great oneyers, such as can hold in, such as will
strike sooner than speak, and speak sooner than
drink, and drink sooner than pray: and yet, zounds,
I lie; for they pray continually to their saint, the
commonwealth; or rather, not pray to her, but prey
on her, for they ride up and down on her and make
her their boots.

Chamberlain

What, the commonwealth their boots? will she hold
  out water in foul way?

GADSHILL

She will, she will; justice hath liquored her. We
  steal as in a castle, cocksure; we have the receipt
  of fern-seed, we walk invisible.

Chamberlain

Nay, by my faith, I think you are more beholding to
  the night than to fern-seed for your walking invisible.

GADSHILL

Give me thy hand: thou shalt have a share in our
  purchase, as I am a true man.

Chamberlain

Nay, rather let me have it, as you are a false thief.

GADSHILL

Go to; 'homo' is a common name to all men. Bid the
  ostler bring my gelding out of the stable. Farewell,
  you muddy knave.

Exeunt

SCENE II. The highway, near Gadshill.

Enter PRINCE HENRY and POINS
POINS
Come, shelter, shelter: I have removed Falstaff's
horse, and he frets like a gummed velvet.
PRINCE HENRY
Stand close.
Enter FALSTAFF
FALSTAFF
Poins! Poins, and be hanged! Poins!
PRINCE HENRY
Peace, ye fat-kidneyed rascal! what a brawling dost
thou keep!
FALSTAFF
Where's Poins, Hal?
PRINCE HENRY
He is walked up to the top of the hill: I'll go seek him.
FALSTAFF
I am accursed to rob in that thief's company: the
rascal hath removed my horse, and tied him I know
not where. If I travel but four foot by the squier
further afoot, I shall break my wind. Well, I doubt
not but to die a fair death for all this, if I
'scape hanging for killing that rogue. I have
forsworn his company hourly any time this two and
twenty years, and yet I am bewitched with the
rogue's company. If the rascal hath not given me
medicines to make me love him, I'll be hanged; it
could not be else: I have drunk medicines. Poins!
Hal! a plague upon you both! Bardolph! Peto!
I'll starve ere I'll rob a foot further. An 'twere
not as good a deed as drink, to turn true man and to
leave these rogues, I am the veriest varlet that
ever chewed with a tooth. Eight yards of uneven
ground is threescore and ten miles afoot with me;
and the stony-hearted villains know it well enough:
a plague upon it when thieves cannot be true one to another!

They whistle

Whew! A plague upon you all! Give me my horse, you
  rogues; give me my horse, and be hanged!

PRINCE HENRY

Peace, ye fat-guts! lie down; lay thine ear close
  to the ground and list if thou canst hear the tread
  of travellers.

FALSTAFF

Have you any levers to lift me up again, being down?
  'Sblood, I'll not bear mine own flesh so far afoot
  again for all the coin in thy father's exchequer.
  What a plague mean ye to colt me thus?

PRINCE HENRY

Thou liest; thou art not colted, thou art uncolted.

FALSTAFF

I prithee, good Prince Hal, help me to my horse,
  good king's son.

PRINCE HENRY

Out, ye rogue! shall I be your ostler?

FALSTAFF

Go, hang thyself in thine own heir-apparent
  garters! If I be ta'en, I'll peach for this. An I
  have not ballads made on you all and sung to filthy
  tunes, let a cup of sack be my poison: when a jest
  is so forward, and afoot too! I hate it.

Enter GADSHILL, BARDOLPH and PETO

GADSHILL

Stand.

FALSTAFF

So I do, against my will.

POINS

O, 'tis our setter: I know his voice. Bardolph,
  what news?

BARDOLPH

Case ye, case ye; on with your vizards: there 's
  money of the king's coming down the hill; 'tis going
  to the king's exchequer.

FALSTAFF

You lie, ye rogue; 'tis going to the king's tavern.

31

GADSHILL

There's enough to make us all.

FALSTAFF

To be hanged.

PRINCE HENRY

Sirs, you four shall front them in the narrow lane;
  Ned Poins and I will walk lower: if they 'scape
  from your encounter, then they light on us.

PETO

How many be there of them?

GADSHILL

Some eight or ten.

FALSTAFF

'Zounds, will they not rob us?

PRINCE HENRY

What, a coward, Sir John Paunch?

FALSTAFF

Indeed, I am not John of Gaunt, your grandfather;
  but yet no coward, Hal.

PRINCE HENRY

Well, we leave that to the proof.

POINS

Sirrah Jack, thy horse stands behind the hedge:
  when thou needest him, there thou shalt find him.
  Farewell, and stand fast.

FALSTAFF

Now cannot I strike him, if I should be hanged.

PRINCE HENRY

Ned, where are our disguises?

POINS

Here, hard by: stand close.

Exeunt PRINCE HENRY and POINS

FALSTAFF

Now, my masters, happy man be his dole, say I:
  every man to his business.

Enter the Travellers

First Traveller

Come, neighbour: the boy shall lead our horses down
  the hill; we'll walk afoot awhile, and ease our legs.

Thieves

Stand!

Travellers

Jesus bless us!

FALSTAFF

Strike; down with them; cut the villains' throats:
 ah! whoreson caterpillars! bacon-fed knaves! they
 hate us youth: down with them: fleece them.

Travellers

O, we are undone, both we and ours for ever!

FALSTAFF

Hang ye, gorbellied knaves, are ye undone? No, ye
 fat chuffs: I would your store were here! On,
 bacons, on! What, ye knaves! young men must live.
 You are Grand-jurors, are ye? we'll jure ye, 'faith.

Here they rob them and bind them. Exeunt
Re-enter PRINCE HENRY and POINS

PRINCE HENRY

The thieves have bound the true men. Now could thou
 and I rob the thieves and go merrily to London, it
 would be argument for a week, laughter for a month
 and a good jest for ever.

POINS

Stand close; I hear them coming.

Enter the Thieves again

FALSTAFF

Come, my masters, let us share, and then to horse
 before day. An the Prince and Poins be not two
 arrant cowards, there's no equity stirring: there's
 no more valour in that Poins than in a wild-duck.

PRINCE HENRY

Your money!

POINS

Villains!

As they are sharing, the Prince and Poins set upon them; they all run away; and
Falstaff, after a blow or two, runs away too, leaving the booty behind them

PRINCE HENRY

Got with much ease. Now merrily to horse:
 The thieves are all scatter'd and possess'd with fear
 So strongly that they dare not meet each other;

Each takes his fellow for an officer.
Away, good Ned. Falstaff sweats to death,
And lards the lean earth as he walks along:
Were 't not for laughing, I should pity him.
  POINS
How the rogue roar'd!
Exeunt

SCENE III. Warkworth castle

Enter HOTSPUR, solus, reading a letter

HOTSPUR

'But for mine own part, my lord, I could be well
contented to be there, in respect of the love I bear
your house.' He could be contented: why is he not,
then? In respect of the love he bears our house:
he shows in this, he loves his own barn better than
he loves our house. Let me see some more. 'The
purpose you undertake is dangerous;'—why, that's
certain: 'tis dangerous to take a cold, to sleep, to
drink; but I tell you, my lord fool, out of this
nettle, danger, we pluck this flower, safety. 'The
purpose you undertake is dangerous; the friends you
have named uncertain; the time itself unsorted; and
your whole plot too light for the counterpoise of so
great an opposition.' Say you so, say you so? I say
unto you again, you are a shallow cowardly hind, and
you lie. What a lack-brain is this! By the Lord,
our plot is a good plot as ever was laid; our
friends true and constant: a good plot, good
friends, and full of expectation; an excellent plot,
very good friends. What a frosty-spirited rogue is
this! Why, my lord of York commends the plot and the
general course of action. 'Zounds, an I were now by
this rascal, I could brain him with his lady's fan.
Is there not my father, my uncle and myself? lord
Edmund Mortimer, My lord of York and Owen Glendower?
is there not besides the Douglas? have I not all
their letters to meet me in arms by the ninth of the
next month? and are they not some of them set
forward already? What a pagan rascal is this! an
infidel! Ha! you shall see now in very sincerity
of fear and cold heart, will he to the king and lay
open all our proceedings. O, I could divide myself
and go to buffets, for moving such a dish of
skim milk with so honourable an action! Hang him!

let him tell the king: we are prepared. I will set
forward to-night.

Enter LADY PERCY

How now, Kate! I must leave you within these two hours.

LADY PERCY

O, my good lord, why are you thus alone?
For what offence have I this fortnight been
A banish'd woman from my Harry's bed?
Tell me, sweet lord, what is't that takes from thee
Thy stomach, pleasure and thy golden sleep?
Why dost thou bend thine eyes upon the earth,
And start so often when thou sit'st alone?
Why hast thou lost the fresh blood in thy cheeks;
And given my treasures and my rights of thee
To thick-eyed musing and cursed melancholy?
In thy faint slumbers I by thee have watch'd,
And heard thee murmur tales of iron wars;
Speak terms of manage to thy bounding steed;
Cry 'Courage! to the field!' And thou hast talk'd
Of sallies and retires, of trenches, tents,
Of palisadoes, frontiers, parapets,
Of basilisks, of cannon, culverin,
Of prisoners' ransom and of soldiers slain,
And all the currents of a heady fight.
Thy spirit within thee hath been so at war
And thus hath so bestirr'd thee in thy sleep,
That beads of sweat have stood upon thy brow
Like bubbles in a late-disturbed stream;
And in thy face strange motions have appear'd,
Such as we see when men restrain their breath
On some great sudden hest. O, what portents are these?
Some heavy business hath my lord in hand,
And I must know it, else he loves me not.

HOTSPUR

What, ho!

Enter Servant

Is Gilliams with the packet gone?

Servant

He is, my lord, an hour ago.

HOTSPUR

Hath Butler brought those horses from the sheriff?

Servant

One horse, my lord, he brought even now.

HOTSPUR

What horse? a roan, a crop-ear, is it not?

Servant

It is, my lord.

HOTSPUR

That roan shall by my throne.
 Well, I will back him straight: O esperance!
 Bid Butler lead him forth into the park.

Exit Servant

LADY PERCY

But hear you, my lord.

HOTSPUR

What say'st thou, my lady?

LADY PERCY

What is it carries you away?

HOTSPUR

Why, my horse, my love, my horse.

LADY PERCY

Out, you mad-headed ape!
 A weasel hath not such a deal of spleen
 As you are toss'd with. In faith,
 I'll know your business, Harry, that I will.
 I fear my brother Mortimer doth stir
 About his title, and hath sent for you
 To line his enterprise: but if you go,—

HOTSPUR

So far afoot, I shall be weary, love.

LADY PERCY

Come, come, you paraquito, answer me
 Directly unto this question that I ask:
 In faith, I'll break thy little finger, Harry,
 An if thou wilt not tell me all things true.

HOTSPUR

Away,
 Away, you trifler! Love! I love thee not,
 I care not for thee, Kate: this is no world

To play with mammets and to tilt with lips:
We must have bloody noses and crack'd crowns,
And pass them current too. God's me, my horse!
What say'st thou, Kate? what would'st thou
have with me?

LADY PERCY

Do you not love me? do you not, indeed?
Well, do not then; for since you love me not,
I will not love myself. Do you not love me?
Nay, tell me if you speak in jest or no.

HOTSPUR

Come, wilt thou see me ride?
And when I am on horseback, I will swear
I love thee infinitely. But hark you, Kate;
I must not have you henceforth question me
Whither I go, nor reason whereabout:
Whither I must, I must; and, to conclude,
This evening must I leave you, gentle Kate.
I know you wise, but yet no farther wise
Than Harry Percy's wife: constant you are,
But yet a woman: and for secrecy,
No lady closer; for I well believe
Thou wilt not utter what thou dost not know;
And so far will I trust thee, gentle Kate.

LADY PERCY

How! so far?

HOTSPUR

Not an inch further. But hark you, Kate:
Whither I go, thither shall you go too;
To-day will I set forth, to-morrow you.
Will this content you, Kate?

LADY PERCY

It must of force.

Exeunt

SCENE IV. The Boar's-Head Tavern, Eastcheap.

Enter PRINCE HENRY and POINS
PRINCE HENRY
Ned, prithee, come out of that fat room, and lend me
thy hand to laugh a little.
POINS
Where hast been, Hal?
PRINCE HENRY
With three or four loggerheads amongst three or four
score hogsheads. I have sounded the very
base-string of humility. Sirrah, I am sworn brother
to a leash of drawers; and can call them all by
their christen names, as Tom, Dick, and Francis.
They take it already upon their salvation, that
though I be but the prince of Wales, yet I am king
of courtesy; and tell me flatly I am no proud Jack,
like Falstaff, but a Corinthian, a lad of mettle, a
good boy, by the Lord, so they call me, and when I
am king of England, I shall command all the good
lads in Eastcheap. They call drinking deep, dyeing
scarlet; and when you breathe in your watering, they
cry 'hem!' and bid you play it off. To conclude, I
am so good a proficient in one quarter of an hour,
that I can drink with any tinker in his own language
during my life. I tell thee, Ned, thou hast lost
much honour, that thou wert not with me in this sweet
action. But, sweet Ned,—to sweeten which name of
Ned, I give thee this pennyworth of sugar, clapped
even now into my hand by an under-skinker, one that
never spake other English in his life than 'Eight
shillings and sixpence' and 'You are welcome,' with
this shrill addition, 'Anon, anon, sir! Score a pint
of bastard in the Half-Moon,' or so. But, Ned, to
drive away the time till Falstaff come, I prithee,
do thou stand in some by-room, while I question my
puny drawer to what end he gave me the sugar; and do
thou never leave calling 'Francis,' that his tale

to me may be nothing but 'Anon.' Step aside, and
I'll show thee a precedent.

POINS

Francis!

PRINCE HENRY

Thou art perfect.

POINS

Francis!

Exit POINS

Enter FRANCIS

FRANCIS

Anon, anon, sir. Look down into the Pomgarnet, Ralph.

PRINCE HENRY

Come hither, Francis.

FRANCIS

My lord?

PRINCE HENRY

How long hast thou to serve, Francis?

FRANCIS

Forsooth, five years, and as much as to—

POINS

[Within] Francis!

FRANCIS

Anon, anon, sir.

PRINCE HENRY

Five year! by'r lady, a long lease for the clinking
 of pewter. But, Francis, darest thou be so valiant
 as to play the coward with thy indenture and show it
 a fair pair of heels and run from it?

FRANCIS

O Lord, sir, I'll be sworn upon all the books in
 England, I could find in my heart.

POINS

[Within] Francis!

FRANCIS

Anon, sir.

PRINCE HENRY

How old art thou, Francis?

FRANCIS

Let me see—about Michaelmas next I shall be—

POINS

[Within] Francis!

FRANCIS

Anon, sir. Pray stay a little, my lord.

PRINCE HENRY

Nay, but hark you, Francis: for the sugar thou
gavest me,'twas a pennyworth, wast't not?

FRANCIS

O Lord, I would it had been two!

PRINCE HENRY

I will give thee for it a thousand pound: ask me
when thou wilt, and thou shalt have it.

POINS

[Within] Francis!

FRANCIS

Anon, anon.

PRINCE HENRY

Anon, Francis? No, Francis; but to-morrow, Francis;
or, Francis, o' Thursday; or indeed, Francis, when
thou wilt. But, Francis!

FRANCIS

My lord?

PRINCE HENRY

Wilt thou rob this leathern jerkin, crystal-button,
not-pated, agate-ring, puke-stocking, caddis-garter,
smooth-tongue, Spanish-pouch,—

FRANCIS

O Lord, sir, who do you mean?

PRINCE HENRY

Why, then, your brown bastard is your only drink;
for look you, Francis, your white canvas doublet
will sully: in Barbary, sir, it cannot come to so much.

FRANCIS

What, sir?

POINS

[Within] Francis!

PRINCE HENRY

Away, you rogue! dost thou not hear them call?

Here they both call him; the drawer stands amazed, not knowing which way to go
Enter Vintner

41

Vintner

What, standest thou still, and hearest such a
 calling? Look to the guests within.
Exit Francis
My lord, old Sir John, with half-a-dozen more, are
 at the door: shall I let them in?

PRINCE HENRY

Let them alone awhile, and then open the door.
Exit Vintner
Poins!
Re-enter POINS

POINS

Anon, anon, sir.

PRINCE HENRY

Sirrah, Falstaff and the rest of the thieves are at
 the door: shall we be merry?

POINS

As merry as crickets, my lad. But hark ye; what
 cunning match have you made with this jest of the
 drawer? come, what's the issue?

PRINCE HENRY

I am now of all humours that have showed themselves
 humours since the old days of goodman Adam to the
 pupil age of this present twelve o'clock at midnight.
Re-enter FRANCIS
What's o'clock, Francis?

FRANCIS

Anon, anon, sir.
Exit

PRINCE HENRY

That ever this fellow should have fewer words than a
 parrot, and yet the son of a woman! His industry is
 upstairs and downstairs; his eloquence the parcel of
 a reckoning. I am not yet of Percy's mind, the
 Hotspur of the north; he that kills me some six or
 seven dozen of Scots at a breakfast, washes his
 hands, and says to his wife 'Fie upon this quiet
 life! I want work.' 'O my sweet Harry,' says she,
 'how many hast thou killed to-day?' 'Give my roan
 horse a drench,' says he; and answers 'Some

fourteen,' an hour after; 'a trifle, a trifle.' I
prithee, call in Falstaff: I'll play Percy, and
that damned brawn shall play Dame Mortimer his
wife. 'Rivo!' says the drunkard. Call in ribs, call in tallow.
Enter FALSTAFF, GADSHILL, BARDOLPH, and PETO; FRANCIS
following with wine

POINS

Welcome, Jack: where hast thou been?

FALSTAFF

A plague of all cowards, I say, and a vengeance too!
marry, and amen! Give me a cup of sack, boy. Ere I
lead this life long, I'll sew nether stocks and mend
them and foot them too. A plague of all cowards!
Give me a cup of sack, rogue. Is there no virtue extant?
He drinks

PRINCE HENRY

Didst thou never see Titan kiss a dish of butter?
pitiful-hearted Titan, that melted at the sweet tale
of the sun's! if thou didst, then behold that compound.

FALSTAFF

You rogue, here's lime in this sack too: there is
nothing but roguery to be found in villanous man:
yet a coward is worse than a cup of sack with lime
in it. A villanous coward! Go thy ways, old Jack;
die when thou wilt, if manhood, good manhood, be
not forgot upon the face of the earth, then am I a
shotten herring. There live not three good men
unhanged in England; and one of them is fat and
grows old: God help the while! a bad world, I say.
I would I were a weaver; I could sing psalms or any
thing. A plague of all cowards, I say still.

PRINCE HENRY

How now, wool-sack! what mutter you?

FALSTAFF

A king's son! If I do not beat thee out of thy
kingdom with a dagger of lath, and drive all thy
subjects afore thee like a flock of wild-geese,
I'll never wear hair on my face more. You Prince of Wales!

PRINCE HENRY

Why, you whoreson round man, what's the matter?

FALSTAFF

Are not you a coward? answer me to that: and Poins there?

POINS

'Zounds, ye fat paunch, an ye call me coward, by the
 Lord, I'll stab thee.

FALSTAFF

I call thee coward! I'll see thee damned ere I call
 thee coward: but I would give a thousand pound I
 could run as fast as thou canst. You are straight
 enough in the shoulders, you care not who sees your
 back: call you that backing of your friends? A
 plague upon such backing! give me them that will
 face me. Give me a cup of sack: I am a rogue, if I
 drunk to-day.

PRINCE HENRY

O villain! thy lips are scarce wiped since thou
 drunkest last.

FALSTAFF

All's one for that.

He drinks

A plague of all cowards, still say I.

PRINCE HENRY

What's the matter?

FALSTAFF

What's the matter! there be four of us here have
 ta'en a thousand pound this day morning.

PRINCE HENRY

Where is it, Jack? where is it?

FALSTAFF

Where is it! taken from us it is: a hundred upon
 poor four of us.

PRINCE HENRY

What, a hundred, man?

FALSTAFF

I am a rogue, if I were not at half-sword with a
 dozen of them two hours together. I have 'scaped by
 miracle. I am eight times thrust through the
 doublet, four through the hose; my buckler cut
 through and through; my sword hacked like a
 hand-saw—ecce signum! I never dealt better since

I was a man: all would not do. A plague of all
cowards! Let them speak: if they speak more or
less than truth, they are villains and the sons of darkness.

PRINCE HENRY

Speak, sirs; how was it?

GADSHILL

We four set upon some dozen—

FALSTAFF

Sixteen at least, my lord.

GADSHILL

And bound them.

PETO

No, no, they were not bound.

FALSTAFF

You rogue, they were bound, every man of them; or I
am a Jew else, an Ebrew Jew.

GADSHILL

As we were sharing, some six or seven fresh men set upon us—

FALSTAFF

And unbound the rest, and then come in the other.

PRINCE HENRY

What, fought you with them all?

FALSTAFF

All! I know not what you call all; but if I fought
not with fifty of them, I am a bunch of radish: if
there were not two or three and fifty upon poor old
Jack, then am I no two-legged creature.

PRINCE HENRY

Pray God you have not murdered some of them.

FALSTAFF

Nay, that's past praying for: I have peppered two
of them; two I am sure I have paid, two rogues
in buckram suits. I tell thee what, Hal, if I tell
thee a lie, spit in my face, call me horse. Thou
knowest my old ward; here I lay and thus I bore my
point. Four rogues in buckram let drive at me—

PRINCE HENRY

What, four? thou saidst but two even now.

FALSTAFF

Four, Hal; I told thee four.

POINS
Ay, ay, he said four.
FALSTAFF
These four came all a-front, and mainly thrust at
me. I made me no more ado but took all their seven
points in my target, thus.
PRINCE HENRY
Seven? why, there were but four even now.
FALSTAFF
In buckram?
POINS
Ay, four, in buckram suits.
FALSTAFF
Seven, by these hilts, or I am a villain else.
PRINCE HENRY
Prithee, let him alone; we shall have more anon.
FALSTAFF
Dost thou hear me, Hal?
PRINCE HENRY
Ay, and mark thee too, Jack.
FALSTAFF
Do so, for it is worth the listening to. These nine
in buckram that I told thee of—
PRINCE HENRY
So, two more already.
FALSTAFF
Their points being broken,—
POINS
Down fell their hose.
FALSTAFF
Began to give me ground: but I followed me close,
came in foot and hand; and with a thought seven of
the eleven I paid.
PRINCE HENRY
O monstrous! eleven buckram men grown out of two!
FALSTAFF
But, as the devil would have it, three misbegotten
knaves in Kendal green came at my back and let drive
at me; for it was so dark, Hal, that thou couldst
not see thy hand.

PRINCE HENRY

These lies are like their father that begets them;
gross as a mountain, open, palpable. Why, thou
clay-brained guts, thou knotty-pated fool, thou
whoreson, obscene, grease tallow-catch,—

FALSTAFF

What, art thou mad? art thou mad? is not the truth
the truth?

PRINCE HENRY

Why, how couldst thou know these men in Kendal
green, when it was so dark thou couldst not see thy
hand? come, tell us your reason: what sayest thou to this?

POINS

Come, your reason, Jack, your reason.

FALSTAFF

What, upon compulsion? 'Zounds, an I were at the
strappado, or all the racks in the world, I would
not tell you on compulsion. Give you a reason on
compulsion! If reasons were as plentiful as
blackberries, I would give no man a reason upon
compulsion, I.

PRINCE HENRY

I'll be no longer guilty of this sin; this sanguine
coward, this bed-presser, this horseback-breaker,
this huge hill of flesh,—

FALSTAFF

'Sblood, you starveling, you elf-skin, you dried
neat's tongue, you bull's pizzle, you stock-fish! O
for breath to utter what is like thee! you
tailor's-yard, you sheath, you bowcase; you vile
standing-tuck,—

PRINCE HENRY

Well, breathe awhile, and then to it again: and
when thou hast tired thyself in base comparisons,
hear me speak but this.

POINS

Mark, Jack.

PRINCE HENRY

We two saw you four set on four and bound them, and
were masters of their wealth. Mark now, how a plain

47

tale shall put you down. Then did we two set on you four; and, with a word, out-faced you from your prize, and have it; yea, and can show it you here in the house: and, Falstaff, you carried your guts away as nimbly, with as quick dexterity, and roared for mercy and still run and roared, as ever I heard bull-calf. What a slave art thou, to hack thy sword as thou hast done, and then say it was in fight! What trick, what device, what starting-hole, canst thou now find out to hide thee from this open and apparent shame?

POINS

Come, let's hear, Jack; what trick hast thou now?

FALSTAFF

By the Lord, I knew ye as well as he that made ye. Why, hear you, my masters: was it for me to kill the heir-apparent? should I turn upon the true prince? why, thou knowest I am as valiant as Hercules: but beware instinct; the lion will not touch the true prince. Instinct is a great matter; I was now a coward on instinct. I shall think the better of myself and thee during my life; I for a valiant lion, and thou for a true prince. But, by the Lord, lads, I am glad you have the money. Hostess, clap to the doors: watch to-night, pray to-morrow. Gallants, lads, boys, hearts of gold, all the titles of good fellowship come to you! What, shall we be merry? shall we have a play extempore?

PRINCE HENRY

Content; and the argument shall be thy running away.

FALSTAFF

Ah, no more of that, Hal, an thou lovest me!

Enter Hostess

Hostess

O Jesu, my lord the prince!

PRINCE HENRY

How now, my lady the hostess! what sayest thou to me?

Hostess

Marry, my lord, there is a nobleman of the court at
door would speak with you: he says he comes from
your father.

PRINCE HENRY

Give him as much as will make him a royal man, and
send him back again to my mother.

FALSTAFF

What manner of man is he?

Hostess

An old man.

FALSTAFF

What doth gravity out of his bed at midnight? Shall
I give him his answer?

PRINCE HENRY

Prithee, do, Jack.

FALSTAFF

'Faith, and I'll send him packing.

Exit FALSTAFF

PRINCE HENRY

Now, sirs: by'r lady, you fought fair; so did you,
Peto; so did you, Bardolph: you are lions too, you
ran away upon instinct, you will not touch the true
prince; no, fie!

BARDOLPH

'Faith, I ran when I saw others run.

PRINCE HENRY

'Faith, tell me now in earnest, how came Falstaff's
sword so hacked?

PETO

Why, he hacked it with his dagger, and said he would
swear truth out of England but he would make you
believe it was done in fight, and persuaded us to do the like.

BARDOLPH

Yea, and to tickle our noses with spear-grass to
make them bleed, and then to beslubber our garments
with it and swear it was the blood of true men. I
did that I did not this seven year before, I blushed
to hear his monstrous devices.

PRINCE HENRY

O villain, thou stolest a cup of sack eighteen years
ago, and wert taken with the manner, and ever since
thou hast blushed extempore. Thou hadst fire and
sword on thy side, and yet thou rannest away: what
instinct hadst thou for it?

BARDOLPH

My lord, do you see these meteors? do you behold
these exhalations?

PRINCE HENRY

I do.

BARDOLPH

What think you they portend?

PRINCE HENRY

Hot livers and cold purses.

BARDOLPH

Choler, my lord, if rightly taken.

PRINCE HENRY

No, if rightly taken, halter.

Re-enter FALSTAFF

Here comes lean Jack, here comes bare-bone.
How now, my sweet creature of bombast!
How long is't ago, Jack, since thou sawest thine own knee?

FALSTAFF

My own knee! when I was about thy years, Hal, I was
not an eagle's talon in the waist; I could have
crept into any alderman's thumb-ring: a plague of
sighing and grief! it blows a man up like a
bladder. There's villanous news abroad: here was
Sir John Bracy from your father; you must to the
court in the morning. That same mad fellow of the
north, Percy, and he of Wales, that gave Amamon the
bastinado and made Lucifer cuckold and swore the
devil his true liegeman upon the cross of a Welsh
hook—what a plague call you him?

POINS

O, Glendower.

FALSTAFF

Owen, Owen, the same; and his son-in-law Mortimer,
and old Northumberland, and that sprightly Scot of

Scots, Douglas, that runs o' horseback up a hill
perpendicular,—

PRINCE HENRY

He that rides at high speed and with his pistol
kills a sparrow flying.

FALSTAFF

You have hit it.

PRINCE HENRY

So did he never the sparrow.

FALSTAFF

Well, that rascal hath good mettle in him; he will not run.

PRINCE HENRY

Why, what a rascal art thou then, to praise him so
for running!

FALSTAFF

O' horseback, ye cuckoo; but afoot he will not budge a foot.

PRINCE HENRY

Yes, Jack, upon instinct.

FALSTAFF

I grant ye, upon instinct. Well, he is there too,
and one Mordake, and a thousand blue-caps more:
Worcester is stolen away to-night; thy father's
beard is turned white with the news: you may buy
land now as cheap as stinking mackerel.

PRINCE HENRY

Why, then, it is like, if there come a hot June and
this civil buffeting hold, we shall buy maidenheads
as they buy hob-nails, by the hundreds.

FALSTAFF

By the mass, lad, thou sayest true; it is like we
shall have good trading that way. But tell me, Hal,
art not thou horrible afeard? thou being
heir-apparent, could the world pick thee out three
such enemies again as that fiend Douglas, that
spirit Percy, and that devil Glendower? Art thou
not horribly afraid? doth not thy blood thrill at
it?

PRINCE HENRY

Not a whit, i' faith; I lack some of thy instinct.

FALSTAFF

Well, thou wert be horribly chid tomorrow when thou
  comest to thy father: if thou love me, practise an answer.

PRINCE HENRY

Do thou stand for my father, and examine me upon the
  particulars of my life.

FALSTAFF

Shall I? content: this chair shall be my state,
  this dagger my sceptre, and this cushion my crown.

PRINCE HENRY

Thy state is taken for a joined-stool, thy golden
  sceptre for a leaden dagger, and thy precious rich
  crown for a pitiful bald crown!

FALSTAFF

Well, an the fire of grace be not quite out of thee,
  now shalt thou be moved. Give me a cup of sack to
  make my eyes look red, that it may be thought I have
  wept; for I must speak in passion, and I will do it
  in King Cambyses' vein.

PRINCE HENRY

Well, here is my leg.

FALSTAFF

And here is my speech. Stand aside, nobility.

Hostess

O Jesu, this is excellent sport, i' faith!

FALSTAFF

Weep not, sweet queen; for trickling tears are vain.

Hostess

O, the father, how he holds his countenance!

FALSTAFF

For God's sake, lords, convey my tristful queen;
  For tears do stop the flood-gates of her eyes.

Hostess

O Jesu, he doth it as like one of these harlotry
  players as ever I see!

FALSTAFF

Peace, good pint-pot; peace, good tickle-brain.
  Harry, I do not only marvel where thou spendest thy
  time, but also how thou art accompanied: for though
  the camomile, the more it is trodden on the faster

it grows, yet youth, the more it is wasted the
sooner it wears. That thou art my son, I have
partly thy mother's word, partly my own opinion,
but chiefly a villanous trick of thine eye and a
foolish-hanging of thy nether lip, that doth warrant
me. If then thou be son to me, here lies the point;
why, being son to me, art thou so pointed at? Shall
the blessed sun of heaven prove a micher and eat
blackberries? a question not to be asked. Shall
the sun of England prove a thief and take purses? a
question to be asked. There is a thing, Harry,
which thou hast often heard of and it is known to
many in our land by the name of pitch: this pitch,
as ancient writers do report, doth defile; so doth
the company thou keepest: for, Harry, now I do not
speak to thee in drink but in tears, not in
pleasure but in passion, not in words only, but in
woes also: and yet there is a virtuous man whom I
have often noted in thy company, but I know not his name.

PRINCE HENRY

What manner of man, an it like your majesty?

FALSTAFF

A goodly portly man, i' faith, and a corpulent; of a
cheerful look, a pleasing eye and a most noble
carriage; and, as I think, his age some fifty, or,
by'r lady, inclining to three score; and now I
remember me, his name is Falstaff: if that man
should be lewdly given, he deceiveth me; for, Harry,
I see virtue in his looks. If then the tree may be
known by the fruit, as the fruit by the tree, then,
peremptorily I speak it, there is virtue in that
Falstaff: him keep with, the rest banish. And tell
me now, thou naughty varlet, tell me, where hast
thou been this month?

PRINCE HENRY

Dost thou speak like a king? Do thou stand for me,
and I'll play my father.

FALSTAFF

Depose me? if thou dost it half so gravely, so
majestically, both in word and matter, hang me up by
the heels for a rabbit-sucker or a poulter's hare.

PRINCE HENRY

Well, here I am set.

FALSTAFF

And here I stand: judge, my masters.

PRINCE HENRY

Now, Harry, whence come you?

FALSTAFF

My noble lord, from Eastcheap.

PRINCE HENRY

The complaints I hear of thee are grievous.

FALSTAFF

'Sblood, my lord, they are false: nay, I'll tickle
ye for a young prince, i' faith.

PRINCE HENRY

Swearest thou, ungracious boy? henceforth ne'er look
on me. Thou art violently carried away from grace:
there is a devil haunts thee in the likeness of an
old fat man; a tun of man is thy companion. Why
dost thou converse with that trunk of humours, that
bolting-hutch of beastliness, that swollen parcel
of dropsies, that huge bombard of sack, that stuffed
cloak-bag of guts, that roasted Manningtree ox with
the pudding in his belly, that reverend vice, that
grey iniquity, that father ruffian, that vanity in
years? Wherein is he good, but to taste sack and
drink it? wherein neat and cleanly, but to carve a
capon and eat it? wherein cunning, but in craft?
wherein crafty, but in villany? wherein villanous,
but in all things? wherein worthy, but in nothing?

FALSTAFF

I would your grace would take me with you: whom
means your grace?

PRINCE HENRY

That villanous abominable misleader of youth,
Falstaff, that old white-bearded Satan.

FALSTAFF

My lord, the man I know.

PRINCE HENRY

I know thou dost.

FALSTAFF

But to say I know more harm in him than in myself,
were to say more than I know. That he is old, the
more the pity, his white hairs do witness it; but
that he is, saving your reverence, a whoremaster,
that I utterly deny. If sack and sugar be a fault,
God help the wicked! if to be old and merry be a
sin, then many an old host that I know is damned: if
to be fat be to be hated, then Pharaoh's lean kine
are to be loved. No, my good lord; banish Peto,
banish Bardolph, banish Poins: but for sweet Jack
Falstaff, kind Jack Falstaff, true Jack Falstaff,
valiant Jack Falstaff, and therefore more valiant,
being, as he is, old Jack Falstaff, banish not him
thy Harry's company, banish not him thy Harry's
company: banish plump Jack, and banish all the world.

PRINCE HENRY

I do, I will.

A knocking heard
Exeunt Hostess, FRANCIS, and BARDOLPH
Re-enter BARDOLPH, running

BARDOLPH

O, my lord, my lord! the sheriff with a most
monstrous watch is at the door.

FALSTAFF

Out, ye rogue! Play out the play: I have much to
say in the behalf of that Falstaff.

Re-enter the Hostess

Hostess

O Jesu, my lord, my lord!

PRINCE HENRY

Heigh, heigh! the devil rides upon a fiddlestick:
what's the matter?

Hostess

The sheriff and all the watch are at the door: they
are come to search the house. Shall I let them in?

FALSTAFF

Dost thou hear, Hal? never call a true piece of
gold a counterfeit: thou art essentially mad,
without seeming so.

PRINCE HENRY

And thou a natural coward, without instinct.

FALSTAFF

I deny your major: if you will deny the sheriff,
so; if not, let him enter: if I become not a cart
as well as another man, a plague on my bringing up!
I hope I shall as soon be strangled with a halter as another.

PRINCE HENRY

Go, hide thee behind the arras: the rest walk up
above. Now, my masters, for a true face and good
conscience.

FALSTAFF

Both which I have had: but their date is out, and
therefore I'll hide me.

PRINCE HENRY

Call in the sheriff.

Exeunt all except PRINCE HENRY and PETO
Enter Sheriff and the Carrier

Now, master sheriff, what is your will with me?

Sheriff

First, pardon me, my lord. A hue and cry
Hath follow'd certain men unto this house.

PRINCE HENRY

What men?

Sheriff

One of them is well known, my gracious lord,
A gross fat man.

Carrier

As fat as butter.

PRINCE HENRY

The man, I do assure you, is not here;
For I myself at this time have employ'd him.
And, sheriff, I will engage my word to thee
That I will, by to-morrow dinner-time,
Send him to answer thee, or any man,

For any thing he shall be charged withal:
And so let me entreat you leave the house.
> **Sheriff**

I will, my lord. There are two gentlemen
Have in this robbery lost three hundred marks.
> **PRINCE HENRY**

It may be so: if he have robb'd these men,
He shall be answerable; and so farewell.
> **Sheriff**

Good night, my noble lord.
> **PRINCE HENRY**

I think it is good morrow, is it not?
> **Sheriff**

Indeed, my lord, I think it be two o'clock.
Exeunt Sheriff and Carrier
> **PRINCE HENRY**

This oily rascal is known as well as Paul's. Go,
call him forth.
> **PETO**

Falstaff!—Fast asleep behind the arras, and
snorting like a horse.
> **PRINCE HENRY**

Hark, how hard he fetches breath. Search his pockets.
He searcheth his pockets, and findeth certain papers
What hast thou found?
> **PETO**

Nothing but papers, my lord.
> **PRINCE HENRY**

Let's see what they be: read them.
> **PETO**

[Reads] Item, A capon,. . 2s. 2d.
Item, Sauce,... 4d.
Item, Sack, two gallons, 5s. 8d.
Item, Anchovies and sack after supper, 2s. 6d.
Item, Bread, ob.
> **PRINCE HENRY**

O monstrous! but one half-penny-worth of bread to
this intolerable deal of sack! What there is else,
keep close; we'll read it at more advantage: there
let him sleep till day. I'll to the court in the

morning. We must all to the wars, and thy place shall be honourable. I'll procure this fat rogue a charge of foot; and I know his death will be a march of twelve-score. The money shall be paid back again with advantage. Be with me betimes in the morning; and so, good morrow, Peto.

Exeunt

PETO

Good morrow, good my lord.

Act III

SCENE I. Bangor. The Archdeacon's house.

Enter HOTSPUR, WORCESTER, MORTIMER, and GLENDOWER

MORTIMER

These promises are fair, the parties sure,
 And our induction full of prosperous hope.

HOTSPUR

Lord Mortimer, and cousin Glendower,
 Will you sit down?
 And uncle Worcester: a plague upon it!
 I have forgot the map.

GLENDOWER

No, here it is.
 Sit, cousin Percy; sit, good cousin Hotspur,
 For by that name as oft as Lancaster
 Doth speak of you, his cheek looks pale and with
 A rising sigh he wisheth you in heaven.

HOTSPUR

And you in hell, as oft as he hears Owen Glendower spoke of.

GLENDOWER

I cannot blame him: at my nativity
 The front of heaven was full of fiery shapes,
 Of burning cressets; and at my birth
 The frame and huge foundation of the earth
 Shaked like a coward.

HOTSPUR

Why, so it would have done at the same season, if
 your mother's cat had but kittened, though yourself
 had never been born.

GLENDOWER

I say the earth did shake when I was born.

HOTSPUR

And I say the earth was not of my mind,
 If you suppose as fearing you it shook.

GLENDOWER

The heavens were all on fire, the earth did tremble.

  HOTSPUR

O, then the earth shook to see the heavens on fire,
 And not in fear of your nativity.
Diseased nature oftentimes breaks forth
In strange eruptions; oft the teeming earth
Is with a kind of colic pinch'd and vex'd
By the imprisoning of unruly wind
Within her womb; which, for enlargement striving,
Shakes the old beldam earth and topples down
Steeples and moss-grown towers. At your birth
Our grandam earth, having this distemperature,
In passion shook.

  GLENDOWER

Cousin, of many men
 I do not bear these crossings. Give me leave
To tell you once again that at my birth
The front of heaven was full of fiery shapes,
The goats ran from the mountains, and the herds
Were strangely clamorous to the frighted fields.
These signs have mark'd me extraordinary;
And all the courses of my life do show
I am not in the roll of common men.
Where is he living, clipp'd in with the sea
 That chides the banks of England, Scotland, Wales,
Which calls me pupil, or hath read to me?
And bring him out that is but woman's son
Can trace me in the tedious ways of art
And hold me pace in deep experiments.

  HOTSPUR

I think there's no man speaks better Welsh.
 I'll to dinner.

  MORTIMER

Peace, cousin Percy; you will make him mad.

  GLENDOWER

I can call spirits from the vasty deep.

  HOTSPUR

Why, so can I, or so can any man;
 But will they come when you do call for them?

GLENDOWER

Why, I can teach you, cousin, to command
The devil.

HOTSPUR

And I can teach thee, coz, to shame the devil
By telling truth: tell truth and shame the devil.
If thou have power to raise him, bring him hither,
And I'll be sworn I have power to shame him hence.
O, while you live, tell truth and shame the devil!

MORTIMER

Come, come, no more of this unprofitable chat.

GLENDOWER

Three times hath Henry Bolingbroke made head
Against my power; thrice from the banks of Wye
And sandy-bottom'd Severn have I sent him
Bootless home and weather-beaten back.

HOTSPUR

Home without boots, and in foul weather too!
How 'scapes he agues, in the devil's name?

GLENDOWER

Come, here's the map: shall we divide our right
According to our threefold order ta'en?

MORTIMER

The archdeacon hath divided it
Into three limits very equally:
England, from Trent and Severn hitherto,
By south and east is to my part assign'd:
All westward, Wales beyond the Severn shore,
And all the fertile land within that bound,
To Owen Glendower: and, dear coz, to you
The remnant northward, lying off from Trent.
And our indentures tripartite are drawn;
Which being sealed interchangeably,
A business that this night may execute,
To-morrow, cousin Percy, you and I
And my good Lord of Worcester will set forth
To meet your father and the Scottish power,
As is appointed us, at Shrewsbury.
My father Glendower is not ready yet,
Not shall we need his help these fourteen days.

Within that space you may have drawn together
Your tenants, friends and neighbouring gentlemen.
 GLENDOWER
A shorter time shall send me to you, lords:
 And in my conduct shall your ladies come;
 From whom you now must steal and take no leave,
For there will be a world of water shed
Upon the parting of your wives and you.
 HOTSPUR
Methinks my moiety, north from Burton here,
 In quantity equals not one of yours:
See how this river comes me cranking in,
And cuts me from the best of all my land
A huge half-moon, a monstrous cantle out.
I'll have the current in this place damm'd up;
And here the smug and silver Trent shall run
In a new channel, fair and evenly;
It shall not wind with such a deep indent,
To rob me of so rich a bottom here.
 GLENDOWER
Not wind? it shall, it must; you see it doth.
 MORTIMER
Yea, but
 Mark how he bears his course, and runs me up
With like advantage on the other side;
Gelding the opposed continent as much
As on the other side it takes from you.
 EARL OF WORCESTER
Yea, but a little charge will trench him here
 And on this north side win this cape of land;
 And then he runs straight and even.
 HOTSPUR
I'll have it so: a little charge will do it.
 GLENDOWER
I'll not have it alter'd.
 HOTSPUR
Will not you?
 GLENDOWER
No, nor you shall not.

HOTSPUR

Who shall say me nay?

GLENDOWER

Why, that will I.

HOTSPUR

Let me not understand you, then; speak it in Welsh.

GLENDOWER

I can speak English, lord, as well as you;
 For I was train'd up in the English court;
 Where, being but young, I framed to the harp
 Many an English ditty lovely well
 And gave the tongue a helpful ornament,
 A virtue that was never seen in you.

HOTSPUR

Marry,
 And I am glad of it with all my heart:
 I had rather be a kitten and cry mew
 Than one of these same metre ballad-mongers;
 I had rather hear a brazen canstick turn'd,
 Or a dry wheel grate on the axle-tree;
 And that would set my teeth nothing on edge,
 Nothing so much as mincing poetry:
 'Tis like the forced gait of a shuffling nag.

GLENDOWER

Come, you shall have Trent turn'd.

HOTSPUR

I do not care: I'll give thrice so much land
 To any well-deserving friend;
 But in the way of bargain, mark ye me,
 I'll cavil on the ninth part of a hair.
 Are the indentures drawn? shall we be gone?

GLENDOWER

The moon shines fair; you may away by night:
 I'll haste the writer and withal
 Break with your wives of your departure hence:
 I am afraid my daughter will run mad,
 So much she doteth on her Mortimer.

Exit GLENDOWER

MORTIMER

Fie, cousin Percy! how you cross my father!

HOTSPUR

I cannot choose: sometime he angers me
With telling me of the mouldwarp and the ant,
Of the dreamer Merlin and his prophecies,
And of a dragon and a finless fish,
A clip-wing'd griffin and a moulten raven,
A couching lion and a ramping cat,
And such a deal of skimble-skamble stuff
As puts me from my faith. I tell you what;
He held me last night at least nine hours
In reckoning up the several devils' names
That were his lackeys: I cried 'hum,' and 'well, go to,'
But mark'd him not a word. O, he is as tedious
As a tired horse, a railing wife;
Worse than a smoky house: I had rather live
With cheese and garlic in a windmill, far,
Than feed on cates and have him talk to me
In any summer-house in Christendom.

MORTIMER

In faith, he is a worthy gentleman,
Exceedingly well read, and profited
In strange concealments, valiant as a lion
And as wondrous affable and as bountiful
As mines of India. Shall I tell you, cousin?
He holds your temper in a high respect
And curbs himself even of his natural scope
When you come 'cross his humour; faith, he does:
I warrant you, that man is not alive
Might so have tempted him as you have done,
Without the taste of danger and reproof:
But do not use it oft, let me entreat you.

EARL OF WORCESTER

In faith, my lord, you are too wilful-blame;
And since your coming hither have done enough
To put him quite beside his patience.
You must needs learn, lord, to amend this fault:
Though sometimes it show greatness, courage, blood,—
And that's the dearest grace it renders you,—
Yet oftentimes it doth present harsh rage,
Defect of manners, want of government,

Pride, haughtiness, opinion and disdain:
The least of which haunting a nobleman
Loseth men's hearts and leaves behind a stain
Upon the beauty of all parts besides,
Beguiling them of commendation.
HOTSPUR
Well, I am school'd: good manners be your speed!
Here come our wives, and let us take our leave.
Re-enter GLENDOWER with the ladies
MORTIMER
This is the deadly spite that angers me;
My wife can speak no English, I no Welsh.
GLENDOWER
My daughter weeps: she will not part with you;
She'll be a soldier too, she'll to the wars.
MORTIMER
Good father, tell her that she and my aunt Percy
Shall follow in your conduct speedily.
Glendower speaks to her in Welsh, and she answers him in the same
GLENDOWER
She is desperate here; a peevish self-wind harlotry,
one that no persuasion can do good upon.
The lady speaks in Welsh
MORTIMER
I understand thy looks: that pretty Welsh
Which thou pour'st down from these swelling heavens
I am too perfect in; and, but for shame,
In such a parley should I answer thee.
The lady speaks again in Welsh
I understand thy kisses and thou mine,
And that's a feeling disputation:
But I will never be a truant, love,
Till I have learned thy language; for thy tongue
Makes Welsh as sweet as ditties highly penn'd,
Sung by a fair queen in a summer's bower,
With ravishing division, to her lute.
GLENDOWER
Nay, if you melt, then will she run mad.
The lady speaks again in Welsh

MORTIMER

O, I am ignorance itself in this!

GLENDOWER

She bids you on the wanton rushes lay you down
  And rest your gentle head upon her lap,
  And she will sing the song that pleaseth you
  And on your eyelids crown the god of sleep.
  Charming your blood with pleasing heaviness,
  Making such difference 'twixt wake and sleep
  As is the difference betwixt day and night
  The hour before the heavenly-harness'd team
  Begins his golden progress in the east.

MORTIMER

With all my heart I'll sit and hear her sing:
  By that time will our book, I think, be drawn

GLENDOWER

Do so;
  And those musicians that shall play to you
  Hang in the air a thousand leagues from hence,
  And straight they shall be here: sit, and attend.

HOTSPUR

Come, Kate, thou art perfect in lying down: come,
  quick, quick, that I may lay my head in thy lap.

LADY PERCY

Go, ye giddy goose.

The music plays

HOTSPUR

Now I perceive the devil understands Welsh;
  And 'tis no marvel he is so humorous.
  By'r lady, he is a good musician.

LADY PERCY

Then should you be nothing but musical for you are
  altogether governed by humours. Lie still, ye thief,
  and hear the lady sing in Welsh.

HOTSPUR

I had rather hear Lady, my brach, howl in Irish.

LADY PERCY

Wouldst thou have thy head broken?

HOTSPUR

No.

LADY PERCY

Then be still.

HOTSPUR

Neither;'tis a woman's fault.

LADY PERCY

Now God help thee!

HOTSPUR

To the Welsh lady's bed.

LADY PERCY

What's that?

HOTSPUR

Peace! she sings.

Here the lady sings a Welsh song

HOTSPUR

Come, Kate, I'll have your song too.

LADY PERCY

Not mine, in good sooth.

HOTSPUR

Not yours, in good sooth! Heart! you swear like a
  comfit-maker's wife. 'Not you, in good sooth,' and
  'as true as I live,' and 'as God shall mend me,' and
  'as sure as day,'
  And givest such sarcenet surety for thy oaths,
  As if thou never walk'st further than Finsbury.
  Swear me, Kate, like a lady as thou art,
  A good mouth-filling oath, and leave 'in sooth,'
  And such protest of pepper-gingerbread,
  To velvet-guards and Sunday-citizens.
  Come, sing.

LADY PERCY

I will not sing.

HOTSPUR

'Tis the next way to turn tailor, or be red-breast
  teacher. An the indentures be drawn, I'll away
  within these two hours; and so, come in when ye will.
Exit

GLENDOWER

Come, come, Lord Mortimer; you are as slow
  As hot Lord Percy is on fire to go.

By this our book is drawn; we'll but seal,
And then to horse immediately.
    MORTIMER
With all my heart.
Exeunt

SCENE II. London. The palace.

Enter KING HENRY IV, PRINCE HENRY, and others
KING HENRY IV
Lords, give us leave; the Prince of Wales and I
 Must have some private conference; but be near at hand,
 For we shall presently have need of you.
Exeunt Lords
I know not whether God will have it so,
 For some displeasing service I have done,
 That, in his secret doom, out of my blood
 He'll breed revengement and a scourge for me;
 But thou dost in thy passages of life
 Make me believe that thou art only mark'd
 For the hot vengeance and the rod of heaven
 To punish my mistreadings. Tell me else,
 Could such inordinate and low desires,
 Such poor, such bare, such lewd, such mean attempts,
 Such barren pleasures, rude society,
 As thou art match'd withal and grafted to,
 Accompany the greatness of thy blood
 And hold their level with thy princely heart?
PRINCE HENRY
So please your majesty, I would I could
 Quit all offences with as clear excuse
 As well as I am doubtless I can purge
 Myself of many I am charged withal:
 Yet such extenuation let me beg,
 As, in reproof of many tales devised,
 which oft the ear of greatness needs must hear,
 By smiling pick-thanks and base news-mongers,
 I may, for some things true, wherein my youth
 Hath faulty wander'd and irregular,
 Find pardon on my true submission.
KING HENRY IV
God pardon thee! yet let me wonder, Harry,
 At thy affections, which do hold a wing
 Quite from the flight of all thy ancestors.

Thy place in council thou hast rudely lost.
Which by thy younger brother is supplied,
And art almost an alien to the hearts
Of all the court and princes of my blood:
The hope and expectation of thy time
Is ruin'd, and the soul of every man
Prophetically doth forethink thy fall.
Had I so lavish of my presence been,
So common-hackney'd in the eyes of men,
So stale and cheap to vulgar company,
Opinion, that did help me to the crown,
Had still kept loyal to possession
And left me in reputeless banishment,
A fellow of no mark nor likelihood.
By being seldom seen, I could not stir
But like a comet I was wonder'd at;
That men would tell their children 'This is he;'
Others would say 'Where, which is Bolingbroke?'
And then I stole all courtesy from heaven,
And dress'd myself in such humility
That I did pluck allegiance from men's hearts,
Loud shouts and salutations from their mouths,
Even in the presence of the crowned king.
Thus did I keep my person fresh and new;
My presence, like a robe pontifical,
Ne'er seen but wonder'd at: and so my state,
Seldom but sumptuous, showed like a feast
And won by rareness such solemnity.
The skipping king, he ambled up and down
With shallow jesters and rash bavin wits,
Soon kindled and soon burnt; carded his state,
Mingled his royalty with capering fools,
Had his great name profaned with their scorns
And gave his countenance, against his name,
To laugh at gibing boys and stand the push
Of every beardless vain comparative,
Grew a companion to the common streets,
Enfeoff'd himself to popularity;
That, being daily swallow'd by men's eyes,
They surfeited with honey and began

To loathe the taste of sweetness, whereof a little
More than a little is by much too much.
So when he had occasion to be seen,
He was but as the cuckoo is in June,
Heard, not regarded; seen, but with such eyes
As, sick and blunted with community,
Afford no extraordinary gaze,
Such as is bent on sun-like majesty
When it shines seldom in admiring eyes;
But rather drowzed and hung their eyelids down,
Slept in his face and render'd such aspect
As cloudy men use to their adversaries,
Being with his presence glutted, gorged and full.
And in that very line, Harry, standest thou;
For thou has lost thy princely privilege
With vile participation: not an eye
But is a-weary of thy common sight,
Save mine, which hath desired to see thee more;
Which now doth that I would not have it do,
Make blind itself with foolish tenderness.

PRINCE HENRY

I shall hereafter, my thrice gracious lord,
Be more myself.

KING HENRY IV

For all the world
As thou art to this hour was Richard then
When I from France set foot at Ravenspurgh,
And even as I was then is Percy now.
Now, by my sceptre and my soul to boot,
He hath more worthy interest to the state
Than thou the shadow of succession;
For of no right, nor colour like to right,
He doth fill fields with harness in the realm,
Turns head against the lion's armed jaws,
And, being no more in debt to years than thou,
Leads ancient lords and reverend bishops on
To bloody battles and to bruising arms.
What never-dying honour hath he got
Against renowned Douglas! whose high deeds,
Whose hot incursions and great name in arms

Holds from all soldiers chief majority
And military title capital
Through all the kingdoms that acknowledge Christ:
Thrice hath this Hotspur, Mars in swathling clothes,
This infant warrior, in his enterprises
Discomfited great Douglas, ta'en him once,
Enlarged him and made a friend of him,
To fill the mouth of deep defiance up
And shake the peace and safety of our throne.
And what say you to this? Percy, Northumberland,
The Archbishop's grace of York, Douglas, Mortimer,
Capitulate against us and are up.
But wherefore do I tell these news to thee?
Why, Harry, do I tell thee of my foes,
Which art my near'st and dearest enemy?
Thou that art like enough, through vassal fear,
Base inclination and the start of spleen
To fight against me under Percy's pay,
To dog his heels and curtsy at his frowns,
To show how much thou art degenerate.

PRINCE HENRY
Do not think so; you shall not find it so:
And God forgive them that so much have sway'd
Your majesty's good thoughts away from me!
I will redeem all this on Percy's head
And in the closing of some glorious day
Be bold to tell you that I am your son;
When I will wear a garment all of blood
And stain my favours in a bloody mask,
Which, wash'd away, shall scour my shame with it:
And that shall be the day, whene'er it lights,
That this same child of honour and renown,
This gallant Hotspur, this all-praised knight,
And your unthought-of Harry chance to meet.
For every honour sitting on his helm,
Would they were multitudes, and on my head
My shames redoubled! for the time will come,
That I shall make this northern youth exchange
His glorious deeds for my indignities.
Percy is but my factor, good my lord,

To engross up glorious deeds on my behalf;
And I will call him to so strict account,
That he shall render every glory up,
Yea, even the slightest worship of his time,
Or I will tear the reckoning from his heart.
This, in the name of God, I promise here:
The which if He be pleased I shall perform,
I do beseech your majesty may salve
The long-grown wounds of my intemperance:
If not, the end of life cancels all bands;
And I will die a hundred thousand deaths
Ere break the smallest parcel of this vow.

KING HENRY IV

A hundred thousand rebels die in this:
 Thou shalt have charge and sovereign trust herein.
Enter BLUNT
How now, good Blunt? thy looks are full of speed.

SIR WALTER BLUNT

So hath the business that I come to speak of.
 Lord Mortimer of Scotland hath sent word
 That Douglas and the English rebels met
 The eleventh of this month at Shrewsbury
 A mighty and a fearful head they are,
 If promises be kept on every hand,
 As ever offer'd foul play in the state.

KING HENRY IV

The Earl of Westmoreland set forth to-day;
 With him my son, Lord John of Lancaster;
 For this advertisement is five days old:
 On Wednesday next, Harry, you shall set forward;
 On Thursday we ourselves will march: our meeting
 Is Bridgenorth: and, Harry, you shall march
 Through Gloucestershire; by which account,
 Our business valued, some twelve days hence
 Our general forces at Bridgenorth shall meet.
 Our hands are full of business: let's away;
 Advantage feeds him fat, while men delay.
Exeunt

Scene III

Eastcheap. The Boar's-Head Tavern.

Enter FALSTAFF and BARDOLPH
   FALSTAFF

Bardolph, am I not fallen away vilely since this last
action? do I not bate? do I not dwindle? Why my
skin hangs about me like an like an old lady's loose
gown; I am withered like an old apple-john. Well,
I'll repent, and that suddenly, while I am in some
liking; I shall be out of heart shortly, and then I
shall have no strength to repent. An I have not
forgotten what the inside of a church is made of, I
am a peppercorn, a brewer's horse: the inside of a
church! Company, villanous company, hath been the
spoil of me.
   BARDOLPH

Sir John, you are so fretful, you cannot live long.
   FALSTAFF

Why, there is it: come sing me a bawdy song; make
me merry. I was as virtuously given as a gentleman
need to be; virtuous enough; swore little; diced not
above seven times a week; went to a bawdy-house once
in a quarter—of an hour; paid money that I
borrowed, three of four times; lived well and in
good compass: and now I live out of all order, out
of all compass.
   BARDOLPH

Why, you are so fat, Sir John, that you must needs
be out of all compass, out of all reasonable
compass, Sir John.
   FALSTAFF

Do thou amend thy face, and I'll amend my life:
thou art our admiral, thou bearest the lantern in
the poop, but 'tis in the nose of thee; thou art the
Knight of the Burning Lamp.
   BARDOLPH

Why, Sir John, my face does you no harm.
   FALSTAFF

No, I'll be sworn; I make as good use of it as many
a man doth of a Death's-head or a memento mori: I
never see thy face but I think upon hell-fire and
Dives that lived in purple; for there he is in his

74

robes, burning, burning. If thou wert any way
given to virtue, I would swear by thy face; my oath
should be 'By this fire, that's God's angel:' but
thou art altogether given over; and wert indeed, but
for the light in thy face, the son of utter
darkness. When thou rannest up Gadshill in the
night to catch my horse, if I did not think thou
hadst been an ignis fatuus or a ball of wildfire,
there's no purchase in money. O, thou art a
perpetual triumph, an everlasting bonfire-light!
Thou hast saved me a thousand marks in links and
torches, walking with thee in the night betwixt
tavern and tavern: but the sack that thou hast
drunk me would have bought me lights as good cheap
at the dearest chandler's in Europe. I have
maintained that salamander of yours with fire any
time this two and thirty years; God reward me for
it!

BARDOLPH

'Sblood, I would my face were in your belly!

FALSTAFF

God-a-mercy! so should I be sure to be heart-burned.
Enter Hostess
How now, Dame Partlet the hen! have you inquired
yet who picked my pocket?

Hostess

Why, Sir John, what do you think, Sir John? do you
think I keep thieves in my house? I have searched,
I have inquired, so has my husband, man by man, boy
by boy, servant by servant: the tithe of a hair
was never lost in my house before.

FALSTAFF

Ye lie, hostess: Bardolph was shaved and lost many
a hair; and I'll be sworn my pocket was picked. Go
to, you are a woman, go.

Hostess

Who, I? no; I defy thee: God's light, I was never
called so in mine own house before.

FALSTAFF

Go to, I know you well enough.

Hostess

No, Sir John; You do not know me, Sir John. I know
you, Sir John: you owe me money, Sir John; and now
you pick a quarrel to beguile me of it: I bought
you a dozen of shirts to your back.

FALSTAFF

Dowlas, filthy dowlas: I have given them away to
bakers' wives, and they have made bolters of them.

Hostess

Now, as I am a true woman, holland of eight
shillings an ell. You owe money here besides, Sir
John, for your diet and by-drinkings, and money lent
you, four and twenty pound.

FALSTAFF

He had his part of it; let him pay.

Hostess

He? alas, he is poor; he hath nothing.

FALSTAFF

How! poor? look upon his face; what call you rich?
let them coin his nose, let them coin his cheeks:
Ill not pay a denier. What, will you make a younker
of me? shall I not take mine case in mine inn but I
shall have my pocket picked? I have lost a
seal-ring of my grandfather's worth forty mark.

Hostess

O Jesu, I have heard the prince tell him, I know not
how oft, that ring was copper!

FALSTAFF

How! the prince is a Jack, a sneak-cup: 'sblood, an
he were here, I would cudgel him like a dog, if he
would say so.

*Enter PRINCE HENRY and PETO, marching, and FALSTAFF meets
them playing on his truncheon like a life*

How now, lad! is the wind in that door, i' faith?
must we all march?

BARDOLPH

Yea, two and two, Newgate fashion.

Hostess

My lord, I pray you, hear me.

PRINCE HENRY

What sayest thou, Mistress Quickly? How doth thy
husband? I love him well; he is an honest man.

Hostess

Good my lord, hear me.

FALSTAFF

Prithee, let her alone, and list to me.

PRINCE HENRY

What sayest thou, Jack?

FALSTAFF

The other night I fell asleep here behind the arras
and had my pocket picked: this house is turned
bawdy-house; they pick pockets.

PRINCE HENRY

What didst thou lose, Jack?

FALSTAFF

Wilt thou believe me, Hal? three or four bonds of
forty pound apiece, and a seal-ring of my
grandfather's.

PRINCE HENRY

A trifle, some eight-penny matter.

Hostess

So I told him, my lord; and I said I heard your
grace say so: and, my lord, he speaks most vilely
of you, like a foul-mouthed man as he is; and said
he would cudgel you.

PRINCE HENRY

What! he did not?

Hostess

There's neither faith, truth, nor womanhood in me else.

FALSTAFF

There's no more faith in thee than in a stewed
prune; nor no more truth in thee than in a drawn
fox; and for womanhood, Maid Marian may be the
deputy's wife of the ward to thee. Go, you thing,
go

Hostess

Say, what thing? what thing?

FALSTAFF

What thing! why, a thing to thank God on.

Hostess

I am no thing to thank God on, I would thou
shouldst know it; I am an honest man's wife: and,
setting thy knighthood aside, thou art a knave to
call me so.

FALSTAFF

Setting thy womanhood aside, thou art a beast to say
otherwise.

Hostess

Say, what beast, thou knave, thou?

FALSTAFF

What beast! why, an otter.

PRINCE HENRY

An otter, Sir John! Why an otter?

FALSTAFF

Why, she's neither fish nor flesh; a man knows not
where to have her.

Hostess

Thou art an unjust man in saying so: thou or any
man knows where to have me, thou knave, thou!

PRINCE HENRY

Thou sayest true, hostess; and he slanders thee most grossly.

Hostess

So he doth you, my lord; and said this other day you
ought him a thousand pound.

PRINCE HENRY

Sirrah, do I owe you a thousand pound?

FALSTAFF

A thousand pound, Ha! a million: thy love is worth
a million: thou owest me thy love.

Hostess

Nay, my lord, he called you Jack, and said he would
cudgel you.

FALSTAFF

Did I, Bardolph?

BARDOLPH

Indeed, Sir John, you said so.

FALSTAFF

Yea, if he said my ring was copper.

PRINCE HENRY

I say 'tis copper: darest thou be as good as thy word now?

FALSTAFF

Why, Hal, thou knowest, as thou art but man, I dare:
but as thou art prince, I fear thee as I fear the
roaring of a lion's whelp.

PRINCE HENRY

And why not as the lion?

FALSTAFF

The king is to be feared as the lion: dost thou
think I'll fear thee as I fear thy father? nay, an
I do, I pray God my girdle break.

PRINCE HENRY

O, if it should, how would thy guts fall about thy
knees! But, sirrah, there's no room for faith,
truth, nor honesty in this bosom of thine; it is all
filled up with guts and midriff. Charge an honest
woman with picking thy pocket! why, thou whoreson,
impudent, embossed rascal, if there were anything in
thy pocket but tavern-reckonings, memorandums of
bawdy-houses, and one poor penny-worth of
sugar-candy to make thee long-winded, if thy pocket
were enriched with any other injuries but these, I
am a villain: and yet you will stand to if; you will
not pocket up wrong: art thou not ashamed?

FALSTAFF

Dost thou hear, Hal? thou knowest in the state of
innocency Adam fell; and what should poor Jack
Falstaff do in the days of villany? Thou seest I
have more flesh than another man, and therefore more
frailty. You confess then, you picked my pocket?

PRINCE HENRY

It appears so by the story.

FALSTAFF

Hostess, I forgive thee: go, make ready breakfast;
love thy husband, look to thy servants, cherish thy
guests: thou shalt find me tractable to any honest
reason: thou seest I am pacified still. Nay,
prithee, be gone.

Exit Hostess

Now Hal, to the news at court: for the robbery,
lad, how is that answered?

PRINCE HENRY

O, my sweet beef, I must still be good angel to
thee: the money is paid back again.

FALSTAFF

O, I do not like that paying back; 'tis a double labour.

PRINCE HENRY

I am good friends with my father and may do any thing.

FALSTAFF

Rob me the exchequer the first thing thou doest, and
do it with unwashed hands too.

BARDOLPH

Do, my lord.

PRINCE HENRY

I have procured thee, Jack, a charge of foot.

FALSTAFF

I would it had been of horse. Where shall I find
one that can steal well? O for a fine thief, of the
age of two and twenty or thereabouts! I am
heinously unprovided. Well, God be thanked for
these rebels, they offend none but the virtuous: I
laud them, I praise them.

PRINCE HENRY

Bardolph!

BARDOLPH

My lord?

PRINCE HENRY

Go bear this letter to Lord John of Lancaster, to my
brother John; this to my Lord of Westmoreland.
Exit Bardolph
Go, Peto, to horse, to horse; for thou and I have
thirty miles to ride yet ere dinner time.
Exit Peto
Jack, meet me to-morrow in the temple hall at two
o'clock in the afternoon.
There shalt thou know thy charge; and there receive
Money and order for their furniture.
The land is burning; Percy stands on high;
And either we or they must lower lie.

Exit PRINCE HENRY
   FALSTAFF
Rare words! brave world! Hostess, my breakfast, come!
 O, I could wish this tavern were my drum!
Exit

Act IV

SCENE I. The rebel camp near Shrewsbury.

Enter HOTSPUR, WORCESTER, and DOUGLAS
HOTSPUR
Well said, my noble Scot: if speaking truth
In this fine age were not thought flattery,
Such attribution should the Douglas have,
As not a soldier of this season's stamp
Should go so general current through the world.
By God, I cannot flatter; I do defy
The tongues of soothers; but a braver place
In my heart's love hath no man than yourself:
Nay, task me to my word; approve me, lord.
EARL OF DOUGLAS
Thou art the king of honour:
No man so potent breathes upon the ground
But I will beard him.
HOTSPUR
Do so, and 'tis well.
Enter a Messenger with letters
What letters hast thou there?—I can but thank you.
Messenger
These letters come from your father.
HOTSPUR
Letters from him! why comes he not himself?
Messenger
He cannot come, my lord; he is grievous sick.
HOTSPUR
'Zounds! how has he the leisure to be sick
In such a rustling time? Who leads his power?
Under whose government come they along?
Messenger
His letters bear his mind, not I, my lord.
EARL OF WORCESTER
I prithee, tell me, doth he keep his bed?

Messenger

He did, my lord, four days ere I set forth;
And at the time of my departure thence
He was much fear'd by his physicians.

EARL OF WORCESTER

I would the state of time had first been whole
Ere he by sickness had been visited:
His health was never better worth than now.

HOTSPUR

Sick now! droop now! this sickness doth infect
The very life-blood of our enterprise;
'Tis catching hither, even to our camp.
He writes me here, that inward sickness—
And that his friends by deputation could not
So soon be drawn, nor did he think it meet
To lay so dangerous and dear a trust
On any soul removed but on his own.
Yet doth he give us bold advertisement,
That with our small conjunction we should on,
To see how fortune is disposed to us;
For, as he writes, there is no quailing now.
Because the king is certainly possess'd
Of all our purposes. What say you to it?

EARL OF WORCESTER

Your father's sickness is a maim to us.

HOTSPUR

A perilous gash, a very limb lopp'd off:
And yet, in faith, it is not; his present want
Seems more than we shall find it: were it good
To set the exact wealth of all our states
All at one cast? to set so rich a main
On the nice hazard of one doubtful hour?
It were not good; for therein should we read
The very bottom and the soul of hope,
The very list, the very utmost bound
Of all our fortunes.

EARL OF DOUGLAS

'Faith, and so we should;
Where now remains a sweet reversion:
We may boldly spend upon the hope of what

83

Is to come in:
A comfort of retirement lives in this.

HOTSPUR

A rendezvous, a home to fly unto.
If that the devil and mischance look big
Upon the maidenhead of our affairs.

EARL OF WORCESTER

But yet I would your father had been here.
The quality and hair of our attempt
Brooks no division: it will be thought
By some, that know not why he is away,
That wisdom, loyalty and mere dislike
Of our proceedings kept the earl from hence:
And think how such an apprehension
May turn the tide of fearful faction
And breed a kind of question in our cause;
For well you know we of the offering side
Must keep aloof from strict arbitrement,
And stop all sight-holes, every loop from whence
The eye of reason may pry in upon us:
This absence of your father's draws a curtain,
That shows the ignorant a kind of fear
Before not dreamt of.

HOTSPUR

You strain too far.
I rather of his absence make this use:
It lends a lustre and more great opinion,
A larger dare to our great enterprise,
Than if the earl were here; for men must think,
If we without his help can make a head
To push against a kingdom, with his help
We shall o'erturn it topsy-turvy down.
Yet all goes well, yet all our joints are whole.

EARL OF DOUGLAS

As heart can think: there is not such a word
Spoke of in Scotland as this term of fear.

Enter SIR RICHARD VERNON

HOTSPUR

My cousin Vernon, welcome, by my soul.

VERNON

Pray God my news be worth a welcome, lord.
The Earl of Westmoreland, seven thousand strong,
Is marching hitherwards; with him Prince John.

HOTSPUR

No harm: what more?

VERNON

And further, I have learn'd,
The king himself in person is set forth,
Or hitherwards intended speedily,
With strong and mighty preparation.

HOTSPUR

He shall be welcome too. Where is his son,
The nimble-footed madcap Prince of Wales,
And his comrades, that daff'd the world aside,
And bid it pass?

VERNON

All furnish'd, all in arms;
All plumed like estridges that with the wind
Baited like eagles having lately bathed;
Glittering in golden coats, like images;
As full of spirit as the month of May,
And gorgeous as the sun at midsummer;
Wanton as youthful goats, wild as young bulls.
I saw young Harry, with his beaver on,
His cuisses on his thighs, gallantly arm'd
Rise from the ground like feather'd Mercury,
And vaulted with such ease into his seat,
As if an angel dropp'd down from the clouds,
To turn and wind a fiery Pegasus
And witch the world with noble horsemanship.

HOTSPUR

No more, no more: worse than the sun in March,
This praise doth nourish agues. Let them come:
They come like sacrifices in their trim,
And to the fire-eyed maid of smoky war
All hot and bleeding will we offer them:
The mailed Mars shall on his altar sit
Up to the ears in blood. I am on fire
To hear this rich reprisal is so nigh

And yet not ours. Come, let me taste my horse,
Who is to bear me like a thunderbolt
Against the bosom of the Prince of Wales:
Harry to Harry shall, hot horse to horse,
Meet and ne'er part till one drop down a corse.
O that Glendower were come!

VERNON

There is more news:
I learn'd in Worcester, as I rode along,
He cannot draw his power this fourteen days.

EARL OF DOUGLAS

That's the worst tidings that I hear of yet.

WORCESTER

Ay, by my faith, that bears a frosty sound.

HOTSPUR

What may the king's whole battle reach unto?

VERNON

To thirty thousand.

HOTSPUR

Forty let it be:
My father and Glendower being both away,
The powers of us may serve so great a day
Come, let us take a muster speedily:
Doomsday is near; die all, die merrily.

EARL OF DOUGLAS

Talk not of dying: I am out of fear
Of death or death's hand for this one-half year.
Exeunt

SCENE II. A public road near Coventry.

Enter FALSTAFF and BARDOLPH

FALSTAFF

Bardolph, get thee before to Coventry; fill me a
bottle of sack: our soldiers shall march through;
we'll to Sutton Co'fil' tonight.

BARDOLPH

Will you give me money, captain?

FALSTAFF

Lay out, lay out.

BARDOLPH

This bottle makes an angel.

FALSTAFF

An if it do, take it for thy labour; and if it make
twenty, take them all; I'll answer the coinage. Bid
my lieutenant Peto meet me at town's end.

BARDOLPH

I will, captain: farewell.

Exit

FALSTAFF

If I be not ashamed of my soldiers, I am a soused
gurnet. I have misused the king's press damnably.
I have got, in exchange of a hundred and fifty
soldiers, three hundred and odd pounds. I press me
none but good house-holders, yeoman's sons; inquire
me out contracted bachelors, such as had been asked
twice on the banns; such a commodity of warm slaves,
as had as lieve hear the devil as a drum; such as
fear the report of a caliver worse than a struck
fowl or a hurt wild-duck. I pressed me none but such
toasts-and-butter, with hearts in their bellies no
bigger than pins' heads, and they have bought out
their services; and now my whole charge consists of
ancients, corporals, lieutenants, gentlemen of
companies, slaves as ragged as Lazarus in the
painted cloth, where the glutton's dogs licked his
sores; and such as indeed were never soldiers, but

discarded unjust serving-men, younger sons to
younger brothers, revolted tapsters and ostlers
trade-fallen, the cankers of a calm world and a
long peace, ten times more dishonourable ragged than
an old faced ancient: and such have I, to fill up
the rooms of them that have bought out their
services, that you would think that I had a hundred
and fifty tattered prodigals lately come from
swine-keeping, from eating draff and husks. A mad
fellow met me on the way and told me I had unloaded
all the gibbets and pressed the dead bodies. No eye
hath seen such scarecrows. I'll not march through
Coventry with them, that's flat: nay, and the
villains march wide betwixt the legs, as if they had
gyves on; for indeed I had the most of them out of
prison. There's but a shirt and a half in all my
company; and the half shirt is two napkins tacked
together and thrown over the shoulders like an
herald's coat without sleeves; and the shirt, to say
the truth, stolen from my host at Saint Alban's, or
the red-nose innkeeper of Daventry. But that's all
one; they'll find linen enough on every hedge.

Enter the PRINCE and WESTMORELAND

PRINCE HENRY

How now, blown Jack! how now, quilt!

FALSTAFF

What, Hal! how now, mad wag! what a devil dost thou
in Warwickshire? My good Lord of Westmoreland, I
cry you mercy: I thought your honour had already been
at Shrewsbury.

WESTMORELAND

Faith, Sir John,'tis more than time that I were
there, and you too; but my powers are there already.
The king, I can tell you, looks for us all: we must
away all night.

FALSTAFF

Tut, never fear me: I am as vigilant as a cat to
steal cream.

PRINCE HENRY

I think, to steal cream indeed, for thy theft hath
already made thee butter. But tell me, Jack, whose
fellows are these that come after?

FALSTAFF

Mine, Hal, mine.

PRINCE HENRY

I did never see such pitiful rascals.

FALSTAFF

Tut, tut; good enough to toss; food for powder, food
for powder; they'll fill a pit as well as better:
tush, man, mortal men, mortal men.

WESTMORELAND

Ay, but, Sir John, methinks they are exceeding poor
and bare, too beggarly.

FALSTAFF

'Faith, for their poverty, I know not where they had
that; and for their bareness, I am sure they never
learned that of me.

PRINCE HENRY

No I'll be sworn; unless you call three fingers on
the ribs bare. But, sirrah, make haste: Percy is
already in the field.

FALSTAFF

What, is the king encamped?

WESTMORELAND

He is, Sir John: I fear we shall stay too long.

FALSTAFF

Well,
To the latter end of a fray and the beginning of a feast
Fits a dull fighter and a keen guest.

Exeunt

SCENE III. The rebel camp near Shrewsbury.

Enter HOTSPUR, WORCESTER, DOUGLAS, and VERNON

HOTSPUR

We'll fight with him to-night.

EARL OF WORCESTER

It may not be.

EARL OF DOUGLAS

You give him then the advantage.

VERNON

Not a whit.

HOTSPUR

Why say you so? looks he not for supply?

VERNON

So do we.

HOTSPUR

His is certain, ours is doubtful.

EARL OF WORCESTER

Good cousin, be advised; stir not tonight.

VERNON

Do not, my lord.

EARL OF DOUGLAS

You do not counsel well:
 You speak it out of fear and cold heart.

VERNON

Do me no slander, Douglas: by my life,
 And I dare well maintain it with my life,
 If well-respected honour bid me on,
 I hold as little counsel with weak fear
 As you, my lord, or any Scot that this day lives:
 Let it be seen to-morrow in the battle
 Which of us fears.

EARL OF DOUGLAS

Yea, or to-night.

VERNON

Content.

HOTSPUR

To-night, say I.

VERNON

Come, come it nay not be. I wonder much,
 Being men of such great leading as you are,
 That you foresee not what impediments
 Drag back our expedition: certain horse
 Of my cousin Vernon's are not yet come up:
 Your uncle Worcester's horse came but today;
 And now their pride and mettle is asleep,
 Their courage with hard labour tame and dull,
 That not a horse is half the half of himself.

HOTSPUR

So are the horses of the enemy
 In general, journey-bated and brought low:
 The better part of ours are full of rest.

EARL OF WORCESTER

The number of the king exceedeth ours:
 For God's sake. cousin, stay till all come in.
The trumpet sounds a parley
Enter SIR WALTER BLUNT

SIR WALTER BLUNT

I come with gracious offers from the king,
 if you vouchsafe me hearing and respect.

HOTSPUR

Welcome, Sir Walter Blunt; and would to God
 You were of our determination!
 Some of us love you well; and even those some
 Envy your great deservings and good name,
 Because you are not of our quality,
 But stand against us like an enemy.

SIR WALTER BLUNT

And God defend but still I should stand so,
 So long as out of limit and true rule
 You stand against anointed majesty.
 But to my charge. The king hath sent to know
 The nature of your griefs, and whereupon
 You conjure from the breast of civil peace
 Such bold hostility, teaching his duteous land
 Audacious cruelty. If that the king
 Have any way your good deserts forgot,
 Which he confesseth to be manifold,

He bids you name your griefs; and with all speed
You shall have your desires with interest
And pardon absolute for yourself and these
Herein misled by your suggestion.

HOTSPUR

The king is kind; and well we know the king
Knows at what time to promise, when to pay.
My father and my uncle and myself
Did give him that same royalty he wears;
And when he was not six and twenty strong,
Sick in the world's regard, wretched and low,
A poor unminded outlaw sneaking home,
My father gave him welcome to the shore;
And when he heard him swear and vow to God
He came but to be Duke of Lancaster,
To sue his livery and beg his peace,
With tears of innocency and terms of zeal,
My father, in kind heart and pity moved,
Swore him assistance and perform'd it too.
Now when the lords and barons of the realm
Perceived Northumberland did lean to him,
The more and less came in with cap and knee;
Met him in boroughs, cities, villages,
Attended him on bridges, stood in lanes,
Laid gifts before him, proffer'd him their oaths,
Gave him their heirs, as pages follow'd him
Even at the heels in golden multitudes.
He presently, as greatness knows itself,
Steps me a little higher than his vow
Made to my father, while his blood was poor,
Upon the naked shore at Ravenspurgh;
And now, forsooth, takes on him to reform
Some certain edicts and some strait decrees
That lie too heavy on the commonwealth,
Cries out upon abuses, seems to weep
Over his country's wrongs; and by this face,
This seeming brow of justice, did he win
The hearts of all that he did angle for;
Proceeded further; cut me off the heads
Of all the favourites that the absent king

In deputation left behind him here,
When he was personal in the Irish war.
SIR WALTER BLUNT
Tut, I came not to hear this.
HOTSPUR
Then to the point.
 In short time after, he deposed the king;
 Soon after that, deprived him of his life;
 And in the neck of that, task'd the whole state:
 To make that worse, suffer'd his kinsman March,
 Who is, if every owner were well placed,
 Indeed his king, to be engaged in Wales,
 There without ransom to lie forfeited;
 Disgraced me in my happy victories,
 Sought to entrap me by intelligence;
 Rated mine uncle from the council-board;
 In rage dismiss'd my father from the court;
 Broke oath on oath, committed wrong on wrong,
 And in conclusion drove us to seek out
 This head of safety; and withal to pry
 Into his title, the which we find
 Too indirect for long continuance.
SIR WALTER BLUNT
Shall I return this answer to the king?
HOTSPUR
Not so, Sir Walter: we'll withdraw awhile.
 Go to the king; and let there be impawn'd
 Some surety for a safe return again,
 And in the morning early shall my uncle
 Bring him our purposes: and so farewell.
SIR WALTER BLUNT
I would you would accept of grace and love.
HOTSPUR
And may be so we shall.
SIR WALTER BLUNT
Pray God you do.
Exeunt

SCENE IV. York. The ARCHBISHOP'S palace.

Enter the ARCHBISHOP OF YORK and SIR MICHAEL
ARCHBISHOP OF YORK
Hie, good Sir Michael; bear this sealed brief
 With winged haste to the lord marshal;
 This to my cousin Scroop, and all the rest
 To whom they are directed. If you knew
 How much they do to import, you would make haste.
SIR MICHAEL
My good lord,
 I guess their tenor.
ARCHBISHOP OF YORK
Like enough you do.
 To-morrow, good Sir Michael, is a day
 Wherein the fortune of ten thousand men
 Must bide the touch; for, sir, at Shrewsbury,
 As I am truly given to understand,
 The king with mighty and quick-raised power
 Meets with Lord Harry: and, I fear, Sir Michael,
 What with the sickness of Northumberland,
 Whose power was in the first proportion,
 And what with Owen Glendower's absence thence,
 Who with them was a rated sinew too
 And comes not in, o'er-ruled by prophecies,
 I fear the power of Percy is too weak
 To wage an instant trial with the king.
SIR MICHAEL
Why, my good lord, you need not fear;
 There is Douglas and Lord Mortimer.
ARCHBISHOP OF YORK
No, Mortimer is not there.
SIR MICHAEL
But there is Mordake, Vernon, Lord Harry Percy,
 And there is my Lord of Worcester and a head
 Of gallant warriors, noble gentlemen.

ARCHBISHOP OF YORK

And so there is: but yet the king hath drawn
 The special head of all the land together:
 The Prince of Wales, Lord John of Lancaster,
 The noble Westmoreland and warlike Blunt;
 And moe corrivals and dear men
 Of estimation and command in arms.

SIR MICHAEL

Doubt not, my lord, they shall be well opposed.

ARCHBISHOP OF YORK

I hope no less, yet needful 'tis to fear;
 And, to prevent the worst, Sir Michael, speed:
 For if Lord Percy thrive not, ere the king
 Dismiss his power, he means to visit us,
 For he hath heard of our confederacy,
 And 'tis but wisdom to make strong against him:
 Therefore make haste. I must go write again
 To other friends; and so farewell, Sir Michael.

Exeunt

Act V

SCENE I. KING HENRY IV's camp near Shrewsbury.

Enter KING HENRY, PRINCE HENRY, Lord John of LANCASTER, EARL OF WESTMORELAND, SIR WALTER BLUNT, and FALSTAFF

KING HENRY IV

How bloodily the sun begins to peer
 Above yon busky hill! the day looks pale
 At his distemperature.

PRINCE HENRY

The southern wind
 Doth play the trumpet to his purposes,
 And by his hollow whistling in the leaves
 Foretells a tempest and a blustering day.

KING HENRY IV

Then with the losers let it sympathize,
 For nothing can seem foul to those that win.

The trumpet sounds

Enter WORCESTER and VERNON

How now, my Lord of Worcester! 'tis not well
 That you and I should meet upon such terms
 As now we meet. You have deceived our trust,
 And made us doff our easy robes of peace,
 To crush our old limbs in ungentle steel:
 This is not well, my lord, this is not well.
 What say you to it? will you again unknit
 This curlish knot of all-abhorred war?
 And move in that obedient orb again
 Where you did give a fair and natural light,
 And be no more an exhaled meteor,
 A prodigy of fear and a portent
 Of broached mischief to the unborn times?

EARL OF WORCESTER

Hear me, my liege:
 For mine own part, I could be well content
 To entertain the lag-end of my life
 With quiet hours; for I do protest,
 I have not sought the day of this dislike.

KING HENRY IV

You have not sought it! how comes it, then?

FALSTAFF

Rebellion lay in his way, and he found it.

PRINCE HENRY

Peace, chewet, peace!

EARL OF WORCESTER

It pleased your majesty to turn your looks
 Of favour from myself and all our house;
 And yet I must remember you, my lord,
 We were the first and dearest of your friends.
 For you my staff of office did I break
 In Richard's time; and posted day and night
 to meet you on the way, and kiss your hand,
 When yet you were in place and in account
 Nothing so strong and fortunate as I.
 It was myself, my brother and his son,
 That brought you home and boldly did outdare
 The dangers of the time. You swore to us,
 And you did swear that oath at Doncaster,
 That you did nothing purpose 'gainst the state;
 Nor claim no further than your new-fall'n right,
 The seat of Gaunt, dukedom of Lancaster:
 To this we swore our aid. But in short space
 It rain'd down fortune showering on your head;
 And such a flood of greatness fell on you,
 What with our help, what with the absent king,
 What with the injuries of a wanton time,
 The seeming sufferances that you had borne,
 And the contrarious winds that held the king
 So long in his unlucky Irish wars
 That all in England did repute him dead:
 And from this swarm of fair advantages
 You took occasion to be quickly woo'd

To gripe the general sway into your hand;
Forget your oath to us at Doncaster;
And being fed by us you used us so
As that ungentle hull, the cuckoo's bird,
Useth the sparrow; did oppress our nest;
Grew by our feeding to so great a bulk
That even our love durst not come near your sight
For fear of swallowing; but with nimble wing
We were enforced, for safety sake, to fly
Out of sight and raise this present head;
Whereby we stand opposed by such means
As you yourself have forged against yourself
By unkind usage, dangerous countenance,
And violation of all faith and troth
Sworn to us in your younger enterprise.

KING HENRY IV

These things indeed you have articulate,
Proclaim'd at market-crosses, read in churches,
To face the garment of rebellion
With some fine colour that may please the eye
Of fickle changelings and poor discontents,
Which gape and rub the elbow at the news
Of hurlyburly innovation:
And never yet did insurrection want
Such water-colours to impaint his cause;
Nor moody beggars, starving for a time
Of pellmell havoc and confusion.

PRINCE HENRY

In both your armies there is many a soul
Shall pay full dearly for this encounter,
If once they join in trial. Tell your nephew,
The Prince of Wales doth join with all the world
In praise of Henry Percy: by my hopes,
This present enterprise set off his head,
I do not think a braver gentleman,
More active-valiant or more valiant-young,
More daring or more bold, is now alive
To grace this latter age with noble deeds.
For my part, I may speak it to my shame,
I have a truant been to chivalry;

And so I hear he doth account me too;
Yet this before my father's majesty—
I am content that he shall take the odds
Of his great name and estimation,
And will, to save the blood on either side,
Try fortune with him in a single fight.

KING HENRY IV

And, Prince of Wales, so dare we venture thee,
Albeit considerations infinite
Do make against it. No, good Worcester, no,
We love our people well; even those we love
That are misled upon your cousin's part;
And, will they take the offer of our grace,
Both he and they and you, every man
Shall be my friend again and I'll be his:
So tell your cousin, and bring me word
What he will do: but if he will not yield,
Rebuke and dread correction wait on us
And they shall do their office. So, be gone;
We will not now be troubled with reply:
We offer fair; take it advisedly.

Exeunt WORCESTER and VERNON

PRINCE HENRY

It will not be accepted, on my life:
The Douglas and the Hotspur both together
Are confident against the world in arms.

KING HENRY IV

Hence, therefore, every leader to his charge;
For, on their answer, will we set on them:
And God befriend us, as our cause is just!

Exeunt all but PRINCE HENRY and FALSTAFF

FALSTAFF

Hal, if thou see me down in the battle and bestride
me, so; 'tis a point of friendship.

PRINCE HENRY

Nothing but a colossus can do thee that friendship.
Say thy prayers, and farewell.

FALSTAFF

I would 'twere bed-time, Hal, and all well.

PRINCE HENRY

Why, thou owest God a death.

Exit PRINCE HENRY

FALSTAFF

'Tis not due yet; I would be loath to pay him before
his day. What need I be so forward with him that
calls not on me? Well, 'tis no matter; honour pricks
me on. Yea, but how if honour prick me off when I
come on? how then? Can honour set to a leg? no: or
an arm? no: or take away the grief of a wound? no.
Honour hath no skill in surgery, then? no. What is
honour? a word. What is in that word honour? what
is that honour? air. A trim reckoning! Who hath it?
he that died o' Wednesday. Doth he feel it? no.
Doth he hear it? no. 'Tis insensible, then. Yea,
to the dead. But will it not live with the living?
no. Why? detraction will not suffer it. Therefore
I'll none of it. Honour is a mere scutcheon: and so
ends my catechism.

Exit

SCENE II. The rebel camp.

Enter WORCESTER and VERNON
EARL OF WORCESTER
O, no, my nephew must not know, Sir Richard,
 The liberal and kind offer of the king.
VERNON
'Twere best he did.
EARL OF WORCESTER
Then are we all undone.
 It is not possible, it cannot be,
 The king should keep his word in loving us;
 He will suspect us still and find a time
 To punish this offence in other faults:
 Suspicion all our lives shall be stuck full of eyes;
 For treason is but trusted like the fox,
 Who, ne'er so tame, so cherish'd and lock'd up,
 Will have a wild trick of his ancestors.
 Look how we can, or sad or merrily,
 Interpretation will misquote our looks,
 And we shall feed like oxen at a stall,
 The better cherish'd, still the nearer death.
 My nephew's trespass may be well forgot;
 it hath the excuse of youth and heat of blood,
 And an adopted name of privilege,
 A hair-brain'd Hotspur, govern'd by a spleen:
 All his offences live upon my head
 And on his father's; we did train him on,
 And, his corruption being ta'en from us,
 We, as the spring of all, shall pay for all.
 Therefore, good cousin, let not Harry know,
 In any case, the offer of the king.
VERNON
Deliver what you will; I'll say 'tis so.
 Here comes your cousin.
Enter HOTSPUR and DOUGLAS

HOTSPUR

My uncle is return'd:
 Deliver up my Lord of Westmoreland.
 Uncle, what news?

EARL OF WORCESTER

The king will bid you battle presently.

EARL OF DOUGLAS

Defy him by the Lord of Westmoreland.

HOTSPUR

Lord Douglas, go you and tell him so.

EARL OF DOUGLAS

Marry, and shall, and very willingly.

Exit

EARL OF WORCESTER

There is no seeming mercy in the king.

HOTSPUR

Did you beg any? God forbid!

EARL OF WORCESTER

I told him gently of our grievances,
 Of his oath-breaking; which he mended thus,
 By now forswearing that he is forsworn:
 He calls us rebels, traitors; and will scourge
 With haughty arms this hateful name in us.

Re-enter the EARL OF DOUGLAS

EARL OF DOUGLAS

Arm, gentlemen; to arms! for I have thrown
 A brave defiance in King Henry's teeth,
 And Westmoreland, that was engaged, did bear it;
 Which cannot choose but bring him quickly on.

EARL OF WORCESTER

The Prince of Wales stepp'd forth before the king,
 And, nephew, challenged you to single fight.

HOTSPUR

O, would the quarrel lay upon our heads,
 And that no man might draw short breath today
 But I and Harry Monmouth! Tell me, tell me,
 How show'd his tasking? seem'd it in contempt?

VERNON

No, by my soul; I never in my life
 Did hear a challenge urged more modestly,

Unless a brother should a brother dare
To gentle exercise and proof of arms.
He gave you all the duties of a man;
Trimm'd up your praises with a princely tongue,
Spoke to your deservings like a chronicle,
Making you ever better than his praise
By still dispraising praise valued in you;
And, which became him like a prince indeed,
He made a blushing cital of himself;
And chid his truant youth with such a grace
As if he master'd there a double spirit.
Of teaching and of learning instantly.
There did he pause: but let me tell the world,
If he outlive the envy of this day,
England did never owe so sweet a hope,
So much misconstrued in his wantonness.
   HOTSPUR
Cousin, I think thou art enamoured
On his follies: never did I hear
Of any prince so wild a libertine.
But be he as he will, yet once ere night
I will embrace him with a soldier's arm,
That he shall shrink under my courtesy.
Arm, arm with speed: and, fellows, soldiers, friends,
Better consider what you have to do
Than I, that have not well the gift of tongue,
Can lift your blood up with persuasion.
Enter a Messenger
   Messenger
My lord, here are letters for you.
   HOTSPUR
I cannot read them now.
O gentlemen, the time of life is short!
To spend that shortness basely were too long,
If life did ride upon a dial's point,
Still ending at the arrival of an hour.
An if we live, we live to tread on kings;
If die, brave death, when princes die with us!
Now, for our consciences, the arms are fair,
When the intent of bearing them is just.

Enter another Messenger
Messenger
My lord, prepare; the king comes on apace.
HOTSPUR
I thank him, that he cuts me from my tale,
For I profess not talking; only this—
Let each man do his best: and here draw I
A sword, whose temper I intend to stain
With the best blood that I can meet withal
In the adventure of this perilous day.
Now, Esperance! Percy! and set on.
Sound all the lofty instruments of war,
And by that music let us all embrace;
For, heaven to earth, some of us never shall
A second time do such a courtesy.
The trumpets sound. They embrace, and exeunt

SCENE III. Plain between the camps.

KING HENRY enters with his power. Alarum to the battle. Then enter DOUGLAS and SIR WALTER BLUNT

SIR WALTER BLUNT

What is thy name, that in the battle thus
 Thou crossest me? what honour dost thou seek
 Upon my head?

EARL OF DOUGLAS

Know then, my name is Douglas;
 And I do haunt thee in the battle thus
 Because some tell me that thou art a king.

SIR WALTER BLUNT

They tell thee true.

EARL OF DOUGLAS

The Lord of Stafford dear to-day hath bought
 Thy likeness, for instead of thee, King Harry,
 This sword hath ended him: so shall it thee,
 Unless thou yield thee as my prisoner.

SIR WALTER BLUNT

I was not born a yielder, thou proud Scot;
 And thou shalt find a king that will revenge
 Lord Stafford's death.

They fight. DOUGLAS kills SIR WALTER BLUNT. Enter HOTSPUR

HOTSPUR

O Douglas, hadst thou fought at Holmedon thus,
 never had triumph'd upon a Scot.

EARL OF DOUGLAS

All's done, all's won; here breathless lies the king.

HOTSPUR

Where?

EARL OF DOUGLAS

Here.

HOTSPUR

This, Douglas? no: I know this face full well:
 A gallant knight he was, his name was Blunt;
 Semblably furnish'd like the king himself.

EARL OF DOUGLAS

A fool go with thy soul, whither it goes!
A borrow'd title hast thou bought too dear:
Why didst thou tell me that thou wert a king?

HOTSPUR

The king hath many marching in his coats.

EARL OF DOUGLAS

Now, by my sword, I will kill all his coats;
I'll murder all his wardrobe, piece by piece,
Until I meet the king.

HOTSPUR

Up, and away!
Our soldiers stand full fairly for the day.

Exeunt

Alarum. Enter FALSTAFF, solus

FALSTAFF

Though I could 'scape shot-free at London, I fear
the shot here; here's no scoring but upon the pate.
Soft! who are you? Sir Walter Blunt: there's honour
for you! here's no vanity! I am as hot as moulten
lead, and as heavy too: God keep lead out of me! I
need no more weight than mine own bowels. I have
led my ragamuffins where they are peppered: there's
not three of my hundred and fifty left alive; and
they are for the town's end, to beg during life.
But who comes here?

Enter PRINCE HENRY

PRINCE HENRY

What, stand'st thou idle here? lend me thy sword:
Many a nobleman lies stark and stiff
Under the hoofs of vaunting enemies,
Whose deaths are yet unrevenged: I prithee,
lend me thy sword.

FALSTAFF

O Hal, I prithee, give me leave to breathe awhile.
Turk Gregory never did such deeds in arms as I have
done this day. I have paid Percy, I have made him sure.

PRINCE HENRY

He is, indeed; and living to kill thee. I prithee,
lend me thy sword.

FALSTAFF

Nay, before God, Hal, if Percy be alive, thou get'st
not my sword; but take my pistol, if thou wilt.

PRINCE HENRY

Give it to me: what, is it in the case?

FALSTAFF

Ay, Hal; 'tis hot, 'tis hot; there's that will sack a city.

PRINCE HENRY draws it out, and finds it to be a bottle of sack

PRINCE HENRY

What, is it a time to jest and dally now?

He throws the bottle at him. Exit

FALSTAFF

Well, if Percy be alive, I'll pierce him. If he do
come in my way, so: if he do not, if I come in his
willingly, let him make a carbonado of me. I like
not such grinning honour as Sir Walter hath: give me
life: which if I can save, so; if not, honour comes
unlooked for, and there's an end.

Exit FALSTAFF

SCENE IV. Another part of the field.

Alarum. Excursions. Enter PRINCE HENRY, LORD JOHN OF LANCASTER, and EARL OF WESTMORELAND

KING HENRY IV

I prithee,
 Harry, withdraw thyself; thou bleed'st too much.
Lord John of Lancaster, go you with him.

LANCASTER

Not I, my lord, unless I did bleed too.

PRINCE HENRY

I beseech your majesty, make up,
 Lest your retirement do amaze your friends.

KING HENRY IV

I will do so.
My Lord of Westmoreland, lead him to his tent.

WESTMORELAND

Come, my lord, I'll lead you to your tent.

PRINCE HENRY

Lead me, my lord? I do not need your help:
 And God forbid a shallow scratch should drive
 The Prince of Wales from such a field as this,
 Where stain'd nobility lies trodden on,
 and rebels' arms triumph in massacres!

LANCASTER

We breathe too long: come, cousin Westmoreland,
 Our duty this way lies; for God's sake come.
Exeunt LANCASTER and WESTMORELAND

PRINCE HENRY

By God, thou hast deceived me, Lancaster;
 I did not think thee lord of such a spirit:
 Before, I loved thee as a brother, John;
 But now, I do respect thee as my soul.

KING HENRY IV

I saw him hold Lord Percy at the point
 With lustier maintenance than I did look for
 Of such an ungrown warrior.

PRINCE HENRY

O, this boy
Lends mettle to us all!

Exit

Enter DOUGLAS

EARL OF DOUGLAS

Another king! they grow like Hydra's heads:
I am the Douglas, fatal to all those
That wear those colours on them: what art thou,
That counterfeit'st the person of a king?

KING HENRY IV

The king himself; who, Douglas, grieves at heart
So many of his shadows thou hast met
And not the very king. I have two boys
Seek Percy and thyself about the field:
But, seeing thou fall'st on me so luckily,
I will assay thee: so, defend thyself.

EARL OF DOUGLAS

I fear thou art another counterfeit;
And yet, in faith, thou bear'st thee like a king:
But mine I am sure thou art, whoe'er thou be,
And thus I win thee.

They fight. KING HENRY being in danger, PRINCE HENRY enters

PRINCE HENRY

Hold up thy head, vile Scot, or thou art like
Never to hold it up again! the spirits
Of valiant Shirley, Stafford, Blunt, are in my arms:
It is the Prince of Wales that threatens thee;
Who never promiseth but he means to pay.

They fight: DOUGLAS flies

Cheerly, my lord how fares your grace?
Sir Nicholas Gawsey hath for succor sent,
And so hath Clifton: I'll to Clifton straight.

KING HENRY IV

Stay, and breathe awhile:
Thou hast redeem'd thy lost opinion,
And show'd thou makest some tender of my life,
In this fair rescue thou hast brought to me.

PRINCE HENRY

O God! they did me too much injury
That ever said I hearken'd for your death.
If it were so, I might have let alone
The insulting hand of Douglas over you,
Which would have been as speedy in your end
As all the poisonous potions in the world
And saved the treacherous labour of your son.

KING HENRY IV

Make up to Clifton: I'll to Sir Nicholas Gawsey.

Exit

Enter HOTSPUR

HOTSPUR

If I mistake not, thou art Harry Monmouth.

PRINCE HENRY

Thou speak'st as if I would deny my name.

HOTSPUR

My name is Harry Percy.

PRINCE HENRY

Why, then I see
A very valiant rebel of the name.
I am the Prince of Wales; and think not, Percy,
To share with me in glory any more:
Two stars keep not their motion in one sphere;
Nor can one England brook a double reign,
Of Harry Percy and the Prince of Wales.

HOTSPUR

Nor shall it, Harry; for the hour is come
To end the one of us; and would to God
Thy name in arms were now as great as mine!

PRINCE HENRY

I'll make it greater ere I part from thee;
And all the budding honours on thy crest
I'll crop, to make a garland for my head.

HOTSPUR

I can no longer brook thy vanities.

They fight

Enter FALSTAFF

FALSTAFF

Well said, Hal! to it Hal! Nay, you shall find no
boy's play here, I can tell you.

*Re-enter DOUGLAS; he fights with FALSTAFF, who falls down as if he were
dead, and exit DOUGLAS. HOTSPUR is wounded, and falls*

HOTSPUR

O, Harry, thou hast robb'd me of my youth!
I better brook the loss of brittle life
Than those proud titles thou hast won of me;
They wound my thoughts worse than sword my flesh:
But thought's the slave of life, and life time's fool;
And time, that takes survey of all the world,
Must have a stop. O, I could prophesy,
But that the earthy and cold hand of death
Lies on my tongue: no, Percy, thou art dust
And food for—

Dies

PRINCE HENRY

For worms, brave Percy: fare thee well, great heart!
Ill-weaved ambition, how much art thou shrunk!
When that this body did contain a spirit,
A kingdom for it was too small a bound;
But now two paces of the vilest earth
Is room enough: this earth that bears thee dead
Bears not alive so stout a gentleman.
If thou wert sensible of courtesy,
I should not make so dear a show of zeal:
But let my favours hide thy mangled face;
And, even in thy behalf, I'll thank myself
For doing these fair rites of tenderness.
Adieu, and take thy praise with thee to heaven!
Thy ignominy sleep with thee in the grave,
But not remember'd in thy epitaph!

He spieth FALSTAFF on the ground

What, old acquaintance! could not all this flesh
Keep in a little life? Poor Jack, farewell!
I could have better spared a better man:
O, I should have a heavy miss of thee,
If I were much in love with vanity!
Death hath not struck so fat a deer to-day,

111

Though many dearer, in this bloody fray.
Embowell'd will I see thee by and by:
Till then in blood by noble Percy lie.
Exit PRINCE HENRY

FALSTAFF

[Rising up] Embowelled! if thou embowel me to-day,
I'll give you leave to powder me and eat me too
to-morrow. 'Sblood,'twas time to counterfeit, or
that hot termagant Scot had paid me scot and lot too.
Counterfeit? I lie, I am no counterfeit: to die,
is to be a counterfeit; for he is but the
counterfeit of a man who hath not the life of a man:
but to counterfeit dying, when a man thereby
liveth, is to be no counterfeit, but the true and
perfect image of life indeed. The better part of
valour is discretion; in the which better part I
have saved my life.'Zounds, I am afraid of this
gunpowder Percy, though he be dead: how, if he
should counterfeit too and rise? by my faith, I am
afraid he would prove the better counterfeit.
Therefore I'll make him sure; yea, and I'll swear I
killed him. Why may not he rise as well as I?
Nothing confutes me but eyes, and nobody sees me.
Therefore, sirrah,
Stabbing him
with a new wound in your thigh, come you along with me.
Takes up HOTSPUR on his back
Re-enter PRINCE HENRY and LORD JOHN OF LANCASTER

PRINCE HENRY

Come, brother John; full bravely hast thou flesh'd
Thy maiden sword.

LANCASTER

But, soft! whom have we here?
Did you not tell me this fat man was dead?

PRINCE HENRY

I did; I saw him dead,
Breathless and bleeding on the ground. Art
thou alive?
Or is it fantasy that plays upon our eyesight?

I prithee, speak; we will not trust our eyes
Without our ears: thou art not what thou seem'st.
>>**FALSTAFF**

No, that's certain; I am not a double man: but if I
be not Jack Falstaff, then am I a Jack. There is Percy:
Throwing the body down
if your father will do me any honour, so; if not, let
him kill the next Percy himself. I look to be either
earl or duke, I can assure you.
>>**PRINCE HENRY**

Why, Percy I killed myself and saw thee dead.
>>**FALSTAFF**

Didst thou? Lord, Lord, how this world is given to
lying! I grant you I was down and out of breath;
and so was he: but we rose both at an instant and
fought a long hour by Shrewsbury clock. If I may be
believed, so; if not, let them that should reward
valour bear the sin upon their own heads. I'll take
it upon my death, I gave him this wound in the
thigh: if the man were alive and would deny it,
'zounds, I would make him eat a piece of my sword.
>>**LANCASTER**

This is the strangest tale that ever I heard.
>>**PRINCE HENRY**

This is the strangest fellow, brother John.
 Come, bring your luggage nobly on your back:
 For my part, if a lie may do thee grace,
 I'll gild it with the happiest terms I have.
A retreat is sounded
The trumpet sounds retreat; the day is ours.
 Come, brother, let us to the highest of the field,
 To see what friends are living, who are dead.
Exeunt PRINCE HENRY and LANCASTER
>>**FALSTAFF**

I'll follow, as they say, for reward. He that
 rewards me, God reward him! If I do grow great,
 I'll grow less; for I'll purge, and leave sack, and
 live cleanly as a nobleman should do.
Exit

SCENE V. Another part of the field.

The trumpets sound. Enter KING HENRY IV, PRINCE HENRY, LORD JOHN LANCASTER, EARL OF WESTMORELAND, with WORCESTER and VERNON prisoners

KING HENRY IV

Thus ever did rebellion find rebuke.
Ill-spirited Worcester! did not we send grace,
Pardon and terms of love to all of you?
And wouldst thou turn our offers contrary?
Misuse the tenor of thy kinsman's trust?
Three knights upon our party slain to-day,
A noble earl and many a creature else
Had been alive this hour,
If like a Christian thou hadst truly borne
Betwixt our armies true intelligence.

EARL OF WORCESTER

What I have done my safety urged me to;
And I embrace this fortune patiently,
Since not to be avoided it falls on me.

KING HENRY IV

Bear Worcester to the death and Vernon too:
Other offenders we will pause upon.
Exeunt WORCESTER and VERNON, guarded
How goes the field?

PRINCE HENRY

The noble Scot, Lord Douglas, when he saw
The fortune of the day quite turn'd from him,
The noble Percy slain, and all his men
Upon the foot of fear, fled with the rest;
And falling from a hill, he was so bruised
That the pursuers took him. At my tent
The Douglas is; and I beseech your grace
I may dispose of him.

KING HENRY IV

With all my heart.

PRINCE HENRY

Then, brother John of Lancaster, to you
This honourable bounty shall belong:
Go to the Douglas, and deliver him
Up to his pleasure, ransomless and free:
His valour shown upon our crests to-day
Hath taught us how to cherish such high deeds
Even in the bosom of our adversaries.

LANCASTER

I thank your grace for this high courtesy,
Which I shall give away immediately.

KING HENRY IV

Then this remains, that we divide our power.
You, son John, and my cousin Westmoreland
Towards York shall bend you with your dearest speed,
To meet Northumberland and the prelate Scroop,
Who, as we hear, are busily in arms:
Myself and you, son Harry, will towards Wales,
To fight with Glendower and the Earl of March.
Rebellion in this land shall lose his sway,
Meeting the cheque of such another day:
And since this business so fair is done,
Let us not leave till all our own be won.

Exeunt

Made in the USA
Lexington, KY
30 August 2018